P9-CEF-253

What people who knew him said:

"Dean died at just the right time. He left behind a legend. If he had lived, he'd never been able to live up to his publicity."

—Humphrey Bogart

"He was a boy with a wonderful sense of the theatre."

—George Stevens

"I still am emotionally unable to watch reruns of *Rebel Without A Cause*. I still talk of Jimmy . . . still find myself thinking of him at odd moments . . ."

—Sal Mineo

"He was a neurotic, mixed-up kid who tried to con everybody to death. There just wasn't an ounce of maturity in that boy."

—Alec Wilder

"With his death, we lost not only a movie star, but a Hamlet, an Orestes, a Peter Gynt—that is an actor who could really act."

—Howard Sackler

THE
JAMES DEAN
STORY
by Ronald Martinetti

PINNACLE BOOKS · NEW YORK CITY

THE JAMES DEAN STORY

Copyright © 1975 by Ronald Martinetti, Inc.

An original Pinnacle Books edition, published for the first time anywhere.

ISBN: 0-523-00633-0

First printing, May 1975

Printed in the United States of America

PINNACLE BOOKS, INC.
275 Madison Avenue
New York, N.Y. 10016

for Andrew Ettinger
and to the memory of
  Lt. Bill Wark
  and for Robert Hubbard,
        Bernard Taper,
        and John S. Gillespie,
        teachers and friends

I would like to specially acknowledge
the help of Rogers Brackett without whose
openness and cooperation this book could
not have been written; and to E. K. who
first suggested the approach.

Introduction

James Dean was little more than a boy when he died, killed at 24 on the highway near Paso Robles, September 30, 1955, while on his way to a sports car meet. At the time of his death Dean had completed three movies, *East of Eden*, *Rebel Without a Cause*, and *Giant*, only the first of which had already been released.

Dean was widely known in Hollywood as a nonconformist, and his death was front-page news. Tributes from admirers poured in to his studio from around the country. A man from Ohio sent $50 for flowers; a woman in New York wrote a poem. By November Warner Brothers was receiving over 200 letters a week, and a year after Dean's death the studio continued to receive up to 8,000 letters a month. "To me he wasn't the late James Dean and never will be," one fan insisted; another wrote: "Dear Jimmy, This is meant to say once and for all how we feel about you . . . We love you."

A special fan-mail agency had to deal with the deluge of mail. Many of the letters asked for photographs, but some requested anything that belonged to Dean, from a lock of his hair to a piece of his demolished car. Actor Nick Adams, Dean's close

1

friend who died from an overdose of drugs in 1968, received letters pleading for a piece of clothing Dean had worn, or even a strip of wallpaper he might have touched. Julie Harris, who costarred with Dean in *East of Eden*, was sent letters wanting to know what it was like to have been kissed by him.

A record, "His Name was Dean," put out on the Forest label, sold 25,000 copies in a single week. Mattson's, a Hollywood clothing shop, received hundreds of orders for red jackets identical to the one Dean had worn in *Rebel Without a Cause*, and Griffith Park, where scenes from the movie were shot, became almost overnight a tourist attraction. Admirers lined up inside the Observatory, hoping to sit in the same seat Dean used in the film. "It's like Valentino," a reporter told Henry Ginsberg, the coproducer of Dean's last movie, referring to the craze that had swept the nation after the Italian actor's death in the 1920's. Ginsberg disagreed. "It's bigger than Valentino."

For young people coming of age in the 1950's—the Eisenhower era—Dean was someone they could easily identify with: an outsider, a loner, Dean was the antithesis of everything a well-behaved youth was supposed to be. His screen portrayals symbolized the rebelliousness of adolescence. In public he was often surly; on the set he was known to have fought with directors. "Jimmy knew what young people were up against," an admirer once said. "He understood." Someone else referred to him as "the first student activist."

Dean's recklessness and commitment to having lived his life to the fullest had its appeal as well. "All adolescents," wrote Martin Mayer in *Esquire*, "want to rope steers . . . and sculpt busts of famous novelists and drive a custom sports car and write poetry and be a great Hollywood star. Dean did it . . . In a way, the kids feel he did it all for them." He was, moreover, the one hero who would never sell out. He would never have a chance to.

Not everyone, however, was enthusiastic about Dean. Herbert Mitgang, the novelist, dismissed him as "an honor graduate of the black leather jacket and motorcycle jackboots school of acting and living it up." And director Elia Kazan, Dean's mentor, claimed: "Every boy goes through a period when he's 17 or so when he hates his father, hates authority, can't live within the rules . . . It's a classic case. Dean just never got out of it."

Still, even two years after Dean's death, Warner Brothers was receiving birthday cards addressed to him, and ultimately the total volume of mail was put at a million pieces. There were reports of kids being unable to concentrate in school because of their preoccupation with Dean, and one fan wrote to a magazine saying that each night she "went to sleep on 16 magazines" containing articles about her idol. These were not isolated incidents, nor were they the most unusual. In San Francisco a Schoolgirl was placed under psychiatric observation because of her obsession with the dead actor, and in Germany two teenagers committed suicide, leaving behind a note, "Jimmy, take us."

"It's crazy," one Hollywood observer told writer Daniel Dixon. "I don't mind telling you the whole thing gives me the creeps."

Some fans refused to believe Dean was really dead. Walter Winchell printed in his column the rumor that

Dean was disfigured but still alive. Other stories insisted that it had been a hitchhiker and not Dean who had been killed, and Dean was in hiding while learning to operate his artificial limbs, or had been placed in a sanatorium.

Fan magazines cashed in on the hysteria, printing articles with titles like "You Can Make Jimmy Dean Live Forever," and "The Boy Who Refuses to Die." One magazine entitled "James Dean Returns," even contained a purported interview with Dean from the beyond.

George Stevens, who directed *Giant*, which was released a year after Dean's death, derided such stories as "morbid nonsense . . . They're trying to make a Bridey Murphy out of him. While he was living, he provoked a little of it. He was a boy with a wonderful sense of the theater."

"A few more films," Stevens added, "and the fans wouldn't have been so bereft. He shortly would have dimmed his luster. The first bright phase would have become an ordinary light and not produced this kind of thing."

Humphrey Bogart, who had known Dean slightly, told journalist Ezra Goodman: "Dean died at just the right time. He left behind a legend. If he had lived, he'd never been able to live up to his publicity."

But Dean did not live, and in death he became transformed into a myth. So much nonsense and so many falsehoods have since been written about him that it is difficult if not impossible to go beneath the legend and write of Dean as he really was, though that is what this book attempts to do.

The complexities in Dean's own nature make the biographer's task all the more difficult. Though he became a symbol of rebellion, Dean himself wanted success and worked hard to attain it. "He wanted success so badly," a relative once said, "that if it didn't come, something inside would have exploded."

Sometimes cruel and arrogant, Dean could also be equally gentle and generous. Once in New York Dean went out of his way to help a young actress land a part in a film he heard was being cast. He hardly knew the girl. "Jimmy didn't have to know you well to do something like that," another actor Rusty Slocum explained.

Yet not all Dean's friends found him loyal. After Dean had achieved success, a struggling young photographer to whom Dean had reason to be grateful asked him to go halves on a used camera. Dean refused. "I can get all the new equipment I want now," he said callously. Dean's half of the bargain would have cost twelve dollars. A biographer is often permitted certain insights into a person's character, but there are some contradictions which perhaps no biographer can adequately explain.

Young females saw in Dean someone to love; males found him a person to admire. "That boy—you know what he did to me?" claimed a woman in her seventies. "He twisted an old tough heart and brought tears. He was like a son—"

But Dean himself was confused by his own identity. "I really don't know who I am," he admitted shortly before his death, "but it really doesn't matter."

Dean was bisexual, though women were strongly attracted to him, and he engaged in numerous affairs. Friends who knew him during his last years in Hollywood claim his relationships were then exclusively heterosexual, and it may be that his early homosexuality was just a passing phase, one more way of his having lived his life to the fullest. Only one of Dean's homosexual relationships is dealt with in this book, and that in his early days in Hollywood with a young director. Whether or not the relationship was only one of convenience for Dean, there is no way of knowing.

Dean's effect on the lives of those who knew him was almost extraordinary. He influenced careers, changed lives, left an impression that was all but indelible. "I still am emotionally unable to watch reruns of *Rebel Without a Cause*," actor Sal Mineo said not long ago. "I still talk of Jimmy with my close friends, still find myself thinking of him at odd moments, still run into complete strangers who ask me to tell them something about Dean."

Not everyone reacted so positively to the young actor. Composer Alec Wilder, who knew Dean well, claims: "He was a neurotic, mixed-up kid who tried to con everybody to death. There just wasn't an ounce of maturity in that boy."

But playwright Howard Sackler, who also knew Dean and who worked with him, expresses another opinion. "With his death, we lost not only a movie star, but a Hamlet, an Orestes, a Peter Gynt—that is, an actor who could really act."

This is his story.

Fame is the thirst of youth
—Byron

Chapter 1

James Byron Dean was born in Marion, Indiana on February 8, 1931. The delivery took place at home in an apartment building on East 4th Street in downtown Marion; at birth Dean weighed eight pounds, ten ounces. The bill was $15.

Dean's father, Winton, was a tall, thin dental technician who worked at the Veteran's Hospital in Marion. The son of a Quaker farmer whose forebears had come to Indiana from Kentucky in 1815, Winton Dean was regarded by his neighbors as a taciturn and serious man. He possessed, as an acquaintance once put it, "the characteristic Dean traits of softness, reticence, and a manner of speaking so slowly and hesitantly that you wanted to prod him with a stick."

Dean's mother, Mildred, also came from a farming background. A short woman, pretty but a bit on the plump side, she had black eyes as sharp and bright as a sparrow's. Around Grant County it was often claimed that her family, the Wilsons, were part Indian; as proof, people pointed to Mildred's eyes. There the evidence ended, but even years later when her son became famous as an actor, someone who worked with him on Broadway dismissed his sometimes wild behavior with the excuse, "He was part Indian, you know." Legends often die hard.

Mildred Dean was a quiet and sensitive girl. Among her neighbors she was thought of as being somewhat distant, and even a bit of a dreamer. "Mildred was never exactly sure what she wanted," a friend in Marion once recalled. "If she bought a new dress on Tuesday, nine times out of ten she'd return it to the store on Wednesday."

Even as a girl Mildred had been deeply interested in the arts, and after her marriage, music and books produced a welcome diversion from the tedium of small-town life. She played the piano well, and was especially fond of poetry.

When her son was born she gave him the romantic-sounding middle name Byron, after her favorite poet, over the mild opposition of her in-laws.

When Dean was four, his father was offered a post as a permanent staff member at the Sawtelle Veteran's Administration Hospital in Los Angeles. After talking it over with his wife, he accepted the job. The family moved to Santa Monica, living in a five-room apartment at 814-B Sixth Street, and the following year Jimmy was enrolled in the Westwood public school system.

Even though the Deans were a young couple struggling to meet the expenses of their new household, Jimmy had all the toys he wanted, and, if anything, seemed to be spoiled beyond his parents' means.

"He had a large anxiety to do many different things," his father later told a magazine writer. "He had to try everything, and he soon outgrew most of the toys we bought him. He always seemed to be getting ahead of himself."

At his mother's insistence Jimmy was given violin

lessons at a very early age. There were also tap dancing classes, and these pursuits, coupled with the fact that he was somewhat undersized for his years, set him apart from other children. At school he had difficulty making friends; his classmates ridiculed his musical studies and teased him about his middle name. He had his share of boyhood fights. Looking back on his early childhood, Dean later chuckled: "I was anemic. I was a goddamn child prodigy."

Mildred Dean never felt comfortable in California. She missed her family back in Indiana and felt isolated in her new surroundings. To a friend visiting from home she confided that she would like to return to Indiana. "Everything's so artificial here," she complained. "I want my son to grow up where things are real and simple."

Although she had been close to her son before, life in California drew them even nearer. She read books to him and devised games which they played by the hour. For one of their games, she built a cardboard theater and, using paper dolls as actors, they took turns making up plays and stories.

Then, in May of 1940, shortly before her 30th birthday, Mildred Dean developed severe chest pains and was hospitalized; her condition was soon diagnosed as cancer.

Winton Dean's mother came from Indiana to help out during the illness. Mildred Dean's chances of recovery were not good, and should the worst occur, Grandmother Dean had come prepared with an offer to take young Jimmy back to Indiana to be raised by relatives. She was in California only seven weeks when Mildred died.

Bereft, deep in doctor's bills from his wife's illness,

Winton Dean agreed with his mother to let Jimmy return with her. At the time he spoke hopefully of sending for his son as soon as he got back on his feet. Eighteen months later, however, he was drafted into the army, and whatever plans he may have had were permanently shattered.

Jimmy and his Grandmother rode east on the same train that carried his mother's body home.

Many years later in Hollywood, after he had made his first movie, Dean blurted out in a famous interview with broadcaster Wally Atkinson, "My mother died on me when I was nine years old. What did she expect, me to do it all by myself?" But to those who knew him best, this loss of his mother was a searing experience, and one he never got over. His chronic insecurity, his need for attention, the searching for a love that always eluded him—all seemed to stem from that terrible and irreparable boyhood experience.

The relatives who welcomed young Jimmy into their home were the Winslows—Winton's sister Ortense and her husband Marcus. Honest, hardworking, they lived on a farm just outside Fairmount, a small town in central Indiana with a population of 2,700.

At the time Jimmy came to live with them they had been married eighteen years and had a daughter, Joan, 14. But they had always wanted a son, too, and eagerly accepted Jimmy into their household; they even gave up their own room and moved across the hall because he liked their maple bedroom furniture.

The Winslow house stands on the edge of a 178-acre parcel of land. A big white house built in 1904, it is situated on top of a small hill, and the land gently rolls down to the farmyard with its white barns and sheds. The farm has sheep, chickens, and pigs; there are some forty acres of oats and long rows of corn. The land here is fertile—the so-called black soil belt of Indiana—and the Winslows' farm yielded a comfortable though modest existence. "We're not rich, but we're not poor either," Grandma Dean said. "So long as I live, I'll always have a porch to sit on, a rocking chair to rock in, and a clock that strikes."

In a short time, as the Winslows had hoped, Jimmy began to fit into the busy routine of farm life. He was given his own chores to do: milking the cows, helping Marcus feed the livestock. It was not long, his cousin Joan recalled, before he was pestering everyone to teach him how to drive the Winslow tractor. Once he learned, he forgot about the tractor and wanted to raise chickens instead. This impetuosity was to remain characteristic his whole life.

In the summers there was swimming in the Winslow pond, fishing for carp, and family picnics. To Uncle Marcus, Jimmy "was a boy, just like any other boy, always chasing some sort of ball . . ." During the winter when the large pond froze over, Jimmy learned to skate, and his uncle rigged up electric lights so that Jimmy and his friends could play hockey at night.

Jimmy also got into his fair share of mischief. "He was always climbing trees and fences he wasn't supposed to climb, and finding new ways of getting into trouble," remembers Helen Walters, a schoolmate. "Once he rigged up an elevator from the top of the barn and nearly broke his neck when the rope snapped. Another time he almost got drowned exploring a fenced-in pothole that was supposed to be bottomless. I guess he was kind of a show-off, but everybody liked him, especially the girls."

On one occasion, trying out a new stunt, Dean lost his four front teeth and had to be fitted for bridgework. He had been swinging on a rope in the Winslow barn, trying to imitate a trapeze artist, and had fallen to the ground. Knowing it made a better story, Dean would sometimes later tell people he had lost his teeth in a motorcycle accident. He had a good imagination, and never hesitated to put it to use.

Jimmy seemed to be a natural actor, a born mimic. At school he could quickly do, with little prodding from his friends, imitations of various teachers; once, when he was in the middle of an impersonation of the school's principal, the man appeared by accident and overheard him. Supposedly, he was so amused by the boy's talent he failed to punish him. Perhaps it is true.

At family gatherings Jimmy would entertain everyone with his mimicry. His family encouraged his talents and liked to speculate that perhaps he took after his great-grandfather Dean, a well-known local auctioneer who was famous for his ability to entertain a crowd while disposing of his wares.

When Jimmy was ten, his aunt asked him to read for a medal at the Women's Christian Temperance Union, an organization in which she was active.

Over the years he won a number of silver and gold medals for his dramatic readings before the WCTU, and Aunt Ortense looked forward to the day when he would compete for the organization's highest award, the pearl bar. "The way they had things," Dean joked, "you could go to hell just for stepping on a grape." But to satisfy his aunt he kept up with the readings.

On the night of the competition for the pearl bar, however, there was a track meet at school that Jimmy wanted to attend instead. His aunt insisted he read for the prize. Reluctantly Jimmy went to the hall, and when his turn came got up before the audience. He stood there several minutes not saying a word, then walked off the stage, to the humiliation of his aunt. Afterwards, he said his mind had gone blank.

"I was sure then of what I had known all along," Ortense said. "You couldn't make James Dean do anything he didn't want to do."

For his thirteenth birthday Jimmy's guardians bought him a Whizzer, a small motorized bike. With the help of his uncle, Dean learned to ride the machine and soon handled it so well that he outgrew it. He traded it for a small used motorcycle of Czech make. "Start an Indiana boy with a jackknife," his grandmother commented proudly, "and he'll end up swapping for a house and lot." By the time Jimmy began high school he had his own full-sized motorcycle.

A favorite hangout of Jimmy's became Marvin Carter's motorcycle shop. Years later, Marvin still remembered the sudden way Dean would come into his shop slightly out of breath, and say, "There's something wrong with my cycle. Can you fix it now?"

If Carter told him no, Jimmy would ride away. "You'd think he was mad as the dickens," Carter added. But five minutes later he would be back again, calmed down. "When can you fix it . . . ?" he would ask.

To Jimmy, waiting was a terrible waste of time; nor was the ability to sit still ever counted among his virtues. When he wasn't pestering Carter with endless questions about whatever machine the mechanic was then working on, he would occupy himself entertaining the other boys who usually crowded the shop. One of them remembers Dean liked to stand at an imaginary public address system, pretending to call out a race. "He'd get us all lined up," he recalls, "tell us what kind of weather it was, who got the jump, who crashed at the first turn, whose motorcycle was bursting into flames. Damned if he didn't make it sound so real, I had to look twice to make sure I wasn't really racing."

To the citizens of Fairmount Dean soon became a familiar sight racing through town astride his machine. "He sounded like a rocket," a store proprietor said. "You could hear him coming three miles away." Dean delighted in doing daredevil feats such as racing while lying flat on the saddle. "If he'd only fallen once, things might have been different," his uncle once reflected. "Trouble is, he never got hurt and he never found anything he couldn't do well almost the first time he tried it. Just one fall off the bike and maybe he'd have been afraid of speed, but he was without fear."

Despite his seemingly outgoing personality, Dean appeared to have few friends, and none that he was close to. "Jimmy considered himself an outsider in town," observed Joe Hyams, a writer who knew him later, "and people in Fairmount quickly regarded him as being different." Unlike most boys his age, commented Hyams, Jimmy "spoke his mind when he felt like it, and he liked to be left alone." Once Dean was expelled from school for fighting with another pupil, Dave Fox. The boy had laughed during a dramatic reading Dean was giving, and this led to a fight outside school. But Dean apologized and was reinstated the next day.

In appearance, Jimmy was thin and on the wiry side; always small for his age, at his full height he stood only 5 feet 8 inches—a fact that studio biographers would always do their best to improve upon. Extremely nearsighted, he was forced to wear thick glasses. "He was blind as a bat without them," an acquaintance said. "I don't think Jimmy ever took them off, not even when he went to bed."

Among his schoolmates Dean bore the added stigma of being virtually an orphan. His father visited him only rarely, and although he had come to call Ortense "Mom," he was always aware that, unlike others at school, he did not live with his real parents.

Then, when Jimmy was fourteen, the Winslows had a son of their own, Marcus, Jr., and suddenly Jimmy was no longer the center of attention in the household. Ortense now had a young baby to care for, and instead of spending all his spare time with Jimmy, Uncle Marcus began sharing it with the two boys.

In his determination to win acceptance, Dean turned to athletics. "I had to prove myself back there," he once said. He began a self-imposed regimen of workouts: running, lifting barbells, copying exercises from a physical fitness book he had bought. In the Winslow barn his uncle had set up a basket, and Dean spent hours alone practicing shooting and learning to dribble the ball.

His efforts paid off well: freshman year at Fairmount High School he made both the basketball and track teams; by sophomore year he earned his letter in baseball as well, playing in the infield.

On the basketball court he became an outstanding player, making up for what he lacked in height with a quick, aggressive style. He broke at least a dozen pairs of glasses, his uncle claimed. Opposing teams soon singled him out as the man to stop.

Although he won the respect of his teammates, Coach Paul Weaver discovered the little guard required special handling. "He wasn't too coachable," Weaver said, a comment directors would echo in the future. "I had to be careful about changing his style of play, and I soon learned not to embarrass him in front of other boys."

In 1948 Dean received his first press notice, an item that appeared in the sports pages of the Fairmount *News*. It called the junior guard "an outstanding threat on the high school team," and mentioned he had "accumulated forty points in three games." Dean's senior year the Fairmount Quakers reached the finals in the sectional tourney, but lost to a tougher team from Marion. In a losing cause, Dean scored fifteen points, a high for both teams.

Having grown bored running the high hurdles on the track team, senior year Dean decided to take up pole vaulting. Mastering this new challenge excited him. "Track," he liked to say, "gave me the sense of discipline I needed." It has always been part of Dean folklore that in his very first meet as a vaulter he broke the existing record for Grant County. But Paul Weaver, who also coached the track team, remembers no such event. The existing record, the coach recalls, was then about 11 feet, and Jimmy's best effort was about 10 feet 6 inches, "a good vault for a high school

16

boy of that time and place." The coach also
remembers Dean as being "quiet, conscientious about
practices, and, like most of the other students, he
always wore blue jeans and a T-shirt. A clean T-shirt."

Outside of school Dean became friendly with a
local Baptist pastor, the Reverend James A. DeWeerd.
Like Dean, Reverend DeWeerd was something of an
outsider in town. Originally from Cincinnati,
DeWeerd was a former army chaplain who had served
in World War II. He had been with the infantry at
Cassino and had suffered a severe shrapnel wound.
For this the army awarded him a Purple Heart as well
as a Silver Star, for gallantry under fire.

Well educated, a man of many interests, DeWeerd
prided himself on his cosmopolitan views. In music
his taste ran to Tchaikovsky, and his conversation was
often sprinkled with quotations from the works of
writers he admired.

In Fairmount he was treated respectfully, although
there were some who didn't know quite what to
make of this stocky preacher who read poetry and
practiced an exotic form of self-discipline called
yoga—it helped, the Reverend explained, ease the
pain of his war injuries.

To Dean DeWeerd became almost a hero. In turn,
DeWeerd sensed in the young boy an inquisitive mind.
"The more you know how to do," the pastor told
him, "and the more things you experience, the better
off you will be."

Under DeWeerd's tutelage, Jimmy's horizons gradually began to broaden. DeWeerd loaned him books
from his library and showed him movies he had taken
on his travels. One evening he showed a film he had
made of a bullfight in Mexico, and Dean was

17

fascinated by it. For the rest of his life bullfighting was to be one of his great passions and one of the few things in which he never lost interest.

From DeWeerd he learned something about music, too, as well as the other arts. He even tried his hand at sculpture, and one afternoon brought a small clay figure to DeWeerd for his approval. The minister carefully studied the work, a four-inch statue of a boy sitting with his head lowered introspectively, his hands covering his face. "It's me," Dean stammered. "I call it *Self*."

To DeWeerd, though, Jimmy was more open than he was with others. He spoke to him about his mother and confessed the guilt he had felt because of her death. DeWeerd did his best to comfort him. "All of us are lonely and searching for answers," DeWeerd later said, "but because he was so sensitive Jimmy was lonelier and searched harder."

When Dean was a senior in high school, DeWeerd taught him to drive a car and took him to Indianapolis to see the famous Memorial Day race, the 500. Dean was thrilled by what he saw and was swept up by the excitement of the crowd and the increasing drama of the afternoon, as the race wore on. All the way back to Fairmount he talked of nothing except the race and Cannonball Baker, a driver he had briefly met.

It was an afternoon DeWeerd would remember grimly when, six years later, Dean perished on his way to just such an event and DeWeerd was asked to conduct a memorial service for his young friend.

In school Dean's interests also began to expand beyond the athletic field. He joined the debating society and was elected president of the Thespians, the school drama club. He played the clarinet in the school band and liked to imitate Benny Goodman, whose records he collected.

"He had a bright mind but didn't always apply himself in high school," his aunt said. "He used to say, 'I'd rather not get good grades than be called a sissy.' But his last year in school he promised he'd make the honor role and he did." Dean received two *A*'s and two *B*'s, one of which was in math, a subject he disliked. Only a lone *C* in U.S. Government marred his report card.

School plays, though, were what interested Dean the most. He played Frankenstein in a Halloween skit, *Goon with the Wind*, and appeared in a production of W.W. Jacob's *The Monkey's Paw*. In the fall of 1947, his junior year, he played the part of Otis Skinner in *Our Hearts Were Young and Gay*. "Whatever ability I may have (as an actor) crystalized back there in high school," Dean said later.

Senior year he tried out for the lead in the school production of the Kaufman and Hart comedy *You Can't Take It with You*, but lost the part to another student, Joe Eliot, who later went to work for a finance company in Marion. Jimmy had to settle for a smaller role, playing a mad Russian.

Students who worked on stage with Dean found him talented—and temperamental. Adeline Nall, who coached the school's drama club and also had Dean in several classes, remembers, "There were times when Jimmy and I were on the outs. We used to squabble when he was my student. We'd always get back together somehow. Once he offered me a cigarette in class just to be smart. I almost popped him. He was just that kind of maverick kid."

At the urging of Miss Nall, Dean decided to enter a contest held by the National Forensic League in March of his senior year. He chose as his selection Charles Dickens' "A Madman's Manuscript" (from *Pickwick Papers*) and stayed after school working with the teacher to polish his reading.

In the state finals held in Peru, Indiana, Dean breezed through and was an easy winner over a student from Culver Military Academy. "I came on stage screaming and tearing at my clothes," Dean said. "Really woke those old judges up."

Accompanied by Miss Nall, Dean traveled to Longmont, Colorado, to compete in the finals.

Longmont is a small, quiet town in the heart of the Rocky Mountains, but it opened its doors gladly to the contestants who poured in from around the country. Students and their faculty representatives boarded with local families, and the town arranged picnics and square dances to help entertain its young guests. For a solid week everyone had a ball; Dean's hosts even allowed him use of the family car.

Dean mingled easily with the others, meeting students from all over. He struck up a friendship with some girls from the South, and within no time was playfully mimicking their accents, to everyone's delight. He also met a young boy his own age from New York, Jim McCarthy, and the two became inseparable.

McCarthy regaled Dean with stories about New York, and Dean listened eagerly to his new friend's tales of crowded streets and night baseball games and even a basketball team called the Globetrotters made up entirely of Negroes who were all wizards with the ball. "Three baseball teams in one town," Dean kept repeating. "Jeez."

Dean was away from home for the first time and enjoying himself, and Miss Nall now found him even harder to handle. In its original presentation, Dean's reading ran twelve minutes, but Miss Nall wanted him to revamp it to run closer to the ten-minute mark the judges now asked for. Dean refused. "We'd go round and round," Miss Nall remembers. "He was a very strong-willed boy."

Dean also refused to wear a coat and tie like the other contestants, instead wanting to appear on stage in jeans and an open shirt. "I can't do the piece if I don't feel it," he said. "How the heck can I go crazy in a suit and tie? It wouldn't work."

Dean won his argument with the teacher, but as she had warned, he did not do well in the contest. The award went to a girl from San Bernardino, California. Dean was not even among the finalists.

Dean was shaken by this setback. On the train back to Fairmount, recalled Miss Nall, he just sulked, hardly saying a word. "He blamed me," she said, "and I blamed him."

Even years later, even after making *East of Eden*, he could not come to grips with the fact that he lost the contest, telling interviewers that after winning the state championship he had not gone on to Colorado. He never quite forgave Miss Nall, either. "That chick was a frustrated actress," he said.

Back in Fairmount, as graduation approached, Dean and his classmates laid plans for the future. Uncle Marcus had hoped that Jimmy might go on to college at his own alma mater, Earlham, a small Quaker school in nearby Richmond, Indiana, and take up agriculture. Jimmy, however, told him he wanted to study acting. The Winslows had heard this before, but had regarded it as another phase Jimmy was going through: in the past he had also spoken of becoming a painter or a lawyer, only to then announce that he had finally settled on medicine. Once he even confided to Miss Nall that he was thinking of entering the ministry. "I wasn't surprised," she said. "He would have made a powerful minister."

But since his return from Longmont acting was all Dean talked about. If he had tasted defeat in Longmont, he had heard the sound of applause too. And it was a sound he liked.

When the Winslows realized he was firm in his intentions, for the present anyway, they decided it would probably be best if he went to school in California; there he could get better training and would be close to his father as well. Winton Dean agreed, writing that he would like Jim in school near him; about his son's plan to study acting he appeared less enthusiastic.

For Jimmy, graduation day, May 16, 1949, was a proud occasion. He graduated in the top half of his class (20th out of 47), and was selected to read a prayer at the end of the graduation ceremonies. The school voted him a medal as best all-around athlete, and he was given a prize by the art department as outstanding student.

Within two weeks, he was packed and ready to leave for California. His diploma and awards were tucked away in the tattered brown suitcase his aunt had given him. He spent the early morning saying goodbye to some friends around town and made a quick last-minute check on his motorcycle, stored in the Winslow tool shed.

His aunt and uncle drove him to the train station. It was early June, but the sun was uncomfortably hot in the Indiana sky. Jimmy seemed not to notice it, talking excitedly as they rode to the station.

He was eighteen, and he was on his way to California to be an actor.

Chapter 2

In California Dean rejoined his father and for a short time everything went fine. Still living in Santa Monica, Winton Dean was now a supervisor at the Veteran's Hospital, having returned to his job after his discharge from the army. He had remarried, in 1945, a woman named Ethel Case, whom he had known before.

Winton Dean was glad to have his son back home, but it soon became apparent that the years of separation had taken their toll. A gap had grown between them that father and son found impossible to bridge. To make matters worse, Jimmy resented his stepmother, and Ethel Case, a proud, strong-willed woman, was quick to sense it.

Over dinner Winton and his son quarrelled frequently over Jimmy's plans for the future. To Winton, acting was "a waste of time," and he urged Jimmy to consider something practical, like law, a field in which he could utilize his talent for public speaking and moreover earn a good living.

In addition, the two disagreed over which college Jimmy should attend in the fall. Jimmy had planned on UCLA, which had an excellent theater department—and a good basketball team too. His father preferred Santa Monica City (now Junior) College, a two-year school, which was closer to home and where tuition was lower.

Things, however, were not all bleak. Jimmy had discovered the existence of a theater group nearby, and was accepted into its ranks. The group was made up mostly of housewives and businessmen, amateur actors drawn together by their love of the theater. They met in the evenings, using whatever facilities they could obtain for their rehearsals.

Dean painted scenery and helped with the props. "I seem to be getting a very cheap theater education," he wrote exuberantly to his aunt and uncle in August. "The work I am doing is easy and advancement is unlimited as to talent . . . (but) we get very little pay if any." He went on to humorously characterize his newfound comrades in the theater as "the most catty, criticizing, narcissistic bunch of people you ever saw, always at each others' throats. But let an outsider try to interfere and they flock together like a bunch of long lost buddies. . . . What a life.

"I learn a lot from them," he added. "I've just got to be patient, I guess. They never made it until their 20's, 30's, and even 40's."

For his efforts backstage, Jimmy was rewarded with a small walk-on role in a musical melodrama called *The Romance of Scarlet Gulch*. In the program he was listed as Byron James, which he then considered adopting permanently as a stage name. For all his feigned sophistication, Jimmy was still a naive young boy, struck by the glamour of the acting profession. At this time Gregory Peck and Jennifer Jones were among his idols. Stanislavski and the

Method meant nothing; the Actors Studio might as well have been on the moon.

In the fall Winton Dean got his wish and Jimmy enrolled in Santa Monica City College. He took a cross-section of required liberal arts courses: English, geology, physics, and Spanish. As an elective he signed up for a class in theater arts.

Santa Monica was a small school with an enrollment of 1600. It had been founded in 1929 and was then located in a temporary cluster of buildings on 7th and Olympic Boulevard while awaiting completion of its new campus across town.

Jimmy found himself very much a big fish in a little pond. He announced for the school's FM radio station and during his first semester was elected to the college Honor Society. He even made the Santa Monica basketball team as a substitute guard. The college belonged to the Metropolitan Conference, playing such opponents as Ventura and Los Angeles City College. Dean got in about half the games. Sanger Crumpacker, the team's coach, remembers him as "a tolerable good guard" and "a leader who went for the ball."

He also found time for dating, and went steady with a girl named Diane Hixon, a willowy blonde who was elected Homecoming Queen.

Dean rooted for the football team, the Corsairs, seldom missing a home game. When several students chartered a bus to San Diego to see the Corsairs play, Dean and Diane went along. Dean had too much to drink at the game and was ill on the ride back.

Since Dean did not have a car, he often double-dated with Larry Swindell, a classmate who owned a black Chevrolet coupe. They often took their dates to The Cave, a dark coffee house frequented by students, or drove out to The Point, a place where they could drink beer overlooking the ocean.

Swindell and Dean were both in the jazz club, and some afternoons they would go down to Ray Avey's Record Roundup, then on La Cienaga Boulevard. Dean liked to pick out old 78's on the Brunswick label. He bought records by Kid Orly, the New Orleans sidegate trombonist, and Frank Trumbauer, the saxophonist who played with the legendary Bix Beiderbecke in Chicago.

Swindell, who is now a book critic on a Philadelphia paper, recalls, "Dean fancied himself as sort of a Renaissance man. He was interested in everything, and had the *idea* that he could do a lot of things well."

Once Dean and Swindell went to hear a lecture, "Is Progress Real?" given by Will Durant at the Santa Monica Auditorium. Durant concluded that indeed much progesss had been made in this century. Dean was very impressed.

Despite all these other activities, however, Dean still found time for his interest in drama. "He would study continually in all areas of dramatics," his teacher, Mrs. Gene N. Owen, recalls, "and was enormously self-educated, a self-starter, and very self-motivated."

Along with classmate Dick Mangan, Dean organized and acted in a May Day production of *She Was Only a Farmer's Daughter*. The show was put on at the Santa Monica Theater Guild. Mangan later acted under the name Richard Shannon and appeared in several Hollywood movies. "Jimmy was like the rainbow," he said. "You don't ever see one color; you see a maze of them. Nothing stands out in my memory of Jimmy but the bright light."

At the end of the year, hoping for bigger game, Dean decided to transfer to UCLA. To help pay his tuition costs Dean worked as an athletic instructor that summer at a boy's camp in Glendora, and in the fall of 1950 entered UCLA as a sophomore.

His major was now listed as theater arts, but again, perhaps as a compromise with his father, he took a cross-section of academic courses: geography, Latin American history, and general anthropology. He also took a course in basic air science as an Air Force ROTC cadet.

To help make friends on the large, sprawling campus, Dean went through rush week and pledged a fraternity, Sigma Nu. He moved into the Sigma Nu house, a rambling English Tudor-style dwelling on Gayley Avenue, and lived in a dorm with eight other pledges.

Jimmy wrote his aunt and uncle, telling them of his fraternity membership, and taking the opportunity to kid his uncle about UCLA's recent upset of Purdue. "You'll have to come West," he told him, "where they really play football."

At the fraternity house, Dean became friendly with Jim Bellah, son of novelist James Warner Bellah. Today a successful novelist himself, author of the *Avenger Tapes*, Bellah was then a theatre arts major who had transferred from Johns Hopkins. He was an ardent fencer and was trying to start a team at UCLA. Dean quickly took up the sport. "The first time he had a foil in his hand he damn near beat me," Bellah recalls. "He was the kind of guy who had to win. He had to be best at everything he did."

This spirit, however, did not endear him to some of the other brothers, and soon they and Dean were at odds. Dean was further criticized for being lax in his pledge duties and chronically late for meals. Manuel Gonzales, the chapter president, remembers: "He spent a great deal of time in individual endeavors rather than taking any part in any cohesive activities. Apparently, he was not comfortable in our group."

Matters came to a head one day when Dean got into a shoving match with another member. Dean later apologized and the incident was temporarily smoothed over, but it was obvious Jimmy's days at Sigma Nu were numbered.

In early October, after a week of auditions, Dean was chosen to play Prince Malcolm in a campus production of *Macbeth*. He described this as "the biggest thrill of my life" in a letter to his aunt and uncle, proudly informing them the play would have almost a week-long run. "God! It's a dream," he wrote. "Don't anyone wake me up."

The part was not large, but it was important, and Dean threw himself into it with his customary enthusiasm—earning the customary response from his fellow actors. "He was egocentric . . ." one complained. "He wouldn't act *with* the rest of us. He always pretended that he was alone on stage." Dr. Walden Boyle, the director, found that Dean wanted "more attention and direction than I could afford to give him in the part."

Rehearsals began on Thursday, October 12. The

play opened at the Royce Hall Auditorium on November 29 and ran through December 2. Tickets for evening performances cost $1.20, matinee seats 60 cents.

Reviewing the production in *Spotlight*, the organ of the theater arts department, critic Harve Bennett Fischman, a former radio Quiz Kid, expressed great disappointment. Fischman wrote: "Void of exciting movement, actor thought processes, and overall conception, the production neither snapped, crackled, nor popped. It just laid there."

Dean's own notice was buried toward the bottom of the page. It was brief and to the point: "Malcolm failed to show any growth and would have made a hollow king." Dean, however, saw things in a different light. Writing to his aunt and uncle in December, he informed them: "The play was very much of a success . . . I was very much rewarded and proved myself a capable actor in the eyes of several hundred culture-minded individuals. Man, if I can keep this up, and nothing interferes with my progress, one of these days I might be able to contribute something to the world (theatrically)."

One evening during rehearsals for *Macbeth* Dean had met William Bast, another student in the theater arts department, who had dropped by to pick up his girlfriend. At first, Bast later recalled, he barely took notice of his new friend; he had seen Dean on stage and had hardly been impressed by his slouching posture and Indiana drawl. James Dean: a name to forget, he decided.

Over coffee, however, the two got to know each other better and discovered their common background. Both were from the Midwest and transfer students. After two years at the University of Wisconsin, Bast had come to UCLA, hoping like Dean to become an actor.

By the time *Macbeth* completed its brief campus run, they were fast friends. It was a friendship that lasted until Dean's death and which Bast recounted in a long and engaging memoir (*James Dean*, Ballantine Books, 1956.)

The two decided to share an apartment off campus, a small three-room flat that Bast accidently happened upon one afternoon. As soon as he showed it to Dean they agreed to take it. To the relief of his fraternity brothers, Dean moved his belongings out of the Sigma Nu house that same afternoon. It was later discovered he left an unpaid bill of $45.

The apartment was conveniently close to campus. Located on the top floor of an old Spanish-style house, it had a slanted, beamed ceiling that sloped from one end of the apartment to the other. There was a chest-high kitchen sink, designed in hard-laid Italian tile, and even a small redwood bar. The décor was all carefully chosen by the landlady, a middle-aged woman with an M.A. degree in art from the University of West Virginia.

Her new tenants quickly put these facilities to good use. Girls from the theater department were invited over to share home-cooked meals, sometimes dining to soft music and candlelight. Things were definitely on the upswing. Frequently, Bast recalled, these informal gatherings lasted well into the night, and one memorable get-together ended when the boys and their dates decided on a whim to drive ninety miles up the coast to have breakfast in Santa Barbara. On the way back the car broke down and they were stranded for several hours along the scenic highway overlooking the Pacific.

All this took its toll on their studies, and the boys' attendance record, which at best had been haphazard, grew worse. As the semester neared its end and exams approached, both Dean and Bast realized they were in serious academic trouble.

Bast was determined to buckle down and get through the welter of term papers and exams that suddenly faced him. Jimmy continued to let things slide. "I wanted to be a professional actor," he said later. "I couldn't take that tea-sipping . . . academic bull." He was undoubtedly telling the truth. The only professor listed on Dean's official transcript, Dr. Joseph B. Birdsell, his anthropology teacher, claims to have no recollection of "a James Dean" as ever having been among his students.

In January Dean wisely decided to withdraw from college, a decision with which university officials concurred. Yet, once his decision to leave school had been made, Dean's spirits lifted. Now at last he could dedicate himself to becoming an actor.

"I don't want to be just a good actor," he told Bast determinedly. "I don't even want to be the best. I want to grow, grow so tall nobody can reach me."

Through Jim Bellah, Dean met an independent theatrical agent, Isabel Draesmer, who had a small office on Sunset Strip. She agreed to take Dean on as a client. She was not the biggest agent in Hollywood, but she was his. Furthermore, in the last few weeks of school Dean's father had gotten him a car: a slightly beat-up and dilapidated 1939 Chevrolet. It was not the sleekest of vehicles, but it ran. And now it would get him to auditions.

Dean's first professional job came deceptively easily. Bellah had heard of a television producer who needed some kids for a Pepsi commercial, and he invited his friend to come along. The commercial was shot in Griffith Park. Dean and the others rode around on a carousel, smiling contentedly. When the director said he also needed an actor to jitterbug in another sequence, Jimmy stepped forward and demonstrated his technique. He got the job and was paid $25 to dance around a jukebox with a pretty girl and a guy named Nick Adams.

In the evenings, Dean started to attend a drama workshop that had been organized by actor James Whitmore at Bill Bast's suggestion.

Whitmore had come to Hollywood after a successful career on Broadway, where he appeared in the play *Command Decision*. Earlier he had studied at the Actors Studio and developed a great admiration and respect for its co-founder Elia Kazan. In Hollywood Whitmore missed both the mental stimulation of New York and the opportunity to seriously study his own art. The idea of starting a class in which he could help young actors to grow, as well as sharpen his own skills, appealed to him at once.

Whitmore's class was informal; students and teacher met two or three times a week, using an abandoned meeting room above the Brentwood Country Mart as a classroom.

"Acting is a craft, a serious profession," Whitmore told his young charges, "and to learn any craft you have to apply yourself. It takes time, study, practice. . . . If it's glory you're after, you won't find it learning to act."

Much of the classwork was rudimentary: concentration techniques, improvisations, all basic exercises. But for the first time Dean and the others became aware that acting was not merely a form of masquerading; it was a process that required you to think and feel deeply.

"You have to work at being an actor," Whitmore kept repeating. "Work until you're ready to drop, and then go on and work some more."

For one improvisation, Dean did a pine tree caught in a storm; he did another together with Bast, in which Dean played a thief who is trapped by a wary jeweler in his store. After an initial unsuccessful run-through, the two did the scene again, this time becoming so involved in their roles they almost came to blows and had to be restrained by other students.

Meanwhile, life back at the penthouse continued apace. Bast was in school again and also working part-time at CBS as an usher to help pay his tuition and support himself. For Dean each day was an endless round of activity: sessions with a photographer to assemble an actor's portfolio, meeting with his agent, auditions.

Even when their second month's rent payment fell due, and the boys were sobered by the dent it made in their resources, they managed to squeeze by without too much sacrifice; meals were more meager, but girls from the theater department were still invited over to share them; dining by candlelight now had even an added charm: It cut down on the utilities bill.

Then, after several discouraging weeks in which nothing came Dean's way, Draesmer sent him and Bellah to audition for a television film being made by the Jerry Fairbanks studio. The film, *Hill Number One*, had a religious theme, and Dean read for the part of John the Apostle, the youngest of Christ's disciples. The casting director was impressed enough to choose Dean at once; Bellah was cast as a Roman soldier. Dean rushed back to the apartment and told Bast the good news, almost tipsy with joy.

An hour-long film, *Hill Number One* was to be taped for local showing during the Easter holidays. It was sponsored by Father Peyton's Family Theater, a well-known Catholic organization whose slogan "The Family that Prays Together Stays Together" had become almost a national byword.

The film's plot was slightly off-beat. Before going into battle, a group of weary GI's in Korea are comforted by a chaplain who narrates the story of Christ's crucifixion on Calvary (Hill Number One). Fortified, the soldiers attack their own objective, Hill Number 46.

The cast was surprisingly noteworthy. Raymond Burr played the Apostle Peter, and Leif Erickson Pontius Pilate. Roddy McDowall was one of the GI's; Ruth Hussey and Gene Lockhart also had roles.

The director, Arthur Pierson, had done a number of Hollywood films, including *Dangerous Years*, which had helped launch the career of Marilyn Monroe.

As the day of shooting approached, Bast remembered, Dean's nervousness increased until it became almost impossible for anyone to be around him. "I sometimes had the feeling," Bast wrote, "that he thought that by talking about the job, or admitting that it even existed, he would lose it. Once or twice it seemed . . . that he was hoarding his pleasure and excitement for fear that I, or someone else, might steal it from him, if he left it unguarded."

The shooting, however, came off well, and the film was completed within the week the studio had allotted for it. Dean was confident he had done a good job; he had one large scene at the end, in which he delivered a speech in front of Christ's tomb, and Arthur Pierson complimented him on his handling of it.

Both Dean and his agent naturally hoped that the film would lead to bigger and better offers, and in the week before it was aired she was busy urging various producers to watch her client's performance. But after the film's release no other offers materialized. The production received several respectful reviews in local papers, and a notice even appeared in *Variety*. It did not mention Dean's name.

The only recognition Dean received was a letter from a group of girls at Immaculate Heart High School in Los Angeles whose teacher had required them to watch the show. They were starting a James Dean fan club, they informed him, and wanted him to be present at their first meeting. Dean went to this meeting and several others the girls held in their homes, before the club quietly disbanded due to lack of funds.

When no new job offers appeared, Dean fell into a state of depression. He would sit in his room for hours, silently staring into space or gazing out the window at the treetops beyond. At night Dean took long walks alone, strolling down to the Venice Amusement Pier to watch the people or walk along the beach, sometimes not returning till dawn.

"If I had thought it difficult to communicate with him at other times," Bast wrote, "I had never known such lack of communication as existed during his fits of depression. For my own peace of mind I found it wise to ignore him, or avoid him completely, going on about my business."

Chapter 3

As summer neared, the enchantment of life in the penthouse grew considerably thinner. The weather turned hot and sticky. The $150 Dean had received for *Hill Number One* was long since used up, and money now became a serious problem.

Girls from the theater department were no longer invited over for dinner. Meals sometimes consisted of a bowl of dry oatmeal mixed with jam preserves; there were days when the larder was completely empty.

Dean managed to overcome his depression sufficiently to resume looking for work. Each morning he would climb into his old Chevy and head into Hollywood, only to return at the end of the day with the same discouraging news. Casting directors told him bluntly he wasn't good-looking enough to make it in the movies, or claimed he was too short to be an actor. "How can you measure acting in inches?" Dean said savagely. "They're crazy."

Luckily, at this time Bill Bast's mother decided to come West for a short visit, and the boys welcomed her presence with open relief. For a week their refrigerator was stocked solid with food, and the cupboard shelves groaned under the weight of newly bought groceries.

For the first time the apartment even appeared orderly, and each night the boys were served a sumptuous meal on the small redwood bar.

After Mrs. Bast departed, Dean decided to find a part-time job to help meet expenses until work as an actor came along. "Jimmy . . . had grown pleasantly accustomed to the little luxuries in life, like food," Bast explained, "and wanted to do something to perpetuate the habits we had formed, like eating."

Bast heartily endorsed his friend's plan, and even arranged an appointment with the head usher at CBS to see about a job. Dean talked to the man and was hired.

From his first day at work, however, Dean found himself in hot water with his new employers. He was overheard complaining about the braided uniform he was given to wear, calling it a "monkey suit," and seemed unable to accord the head usher the proper respect demanded by his rank.

After a week Dean was fired.

"About your friend . . . ," Bast was later chided at CBS, "let me tell you . . ."

As Dean slipped quickly and happily back into the ranks of the unemployed, the boys' financial situation looked bleaker than ever. "Times were still hard," Bast wrote, "and getting harder." Furthermore, Bast was tired of supporting them both, and his resentment grew daily.

To make matters worse, Dean began to spend much of his ample leisure time with a pretty girl, Beverly Wills, to whom Bast had introduced him and whom he occasionally dated himself. The daughter of popular comedienne Joan Davis, Beverly was seventeen and the star of her own weekly CBS radio program, "Junior Miss." She lived with her mother in a mansion in fashionable Bel Air.

Unfortunately, Miss Davis did not share her daughter's enthusiasm for Dean. "He'd walk into our living room," Beverly recalled, "and promptly slump down in my mother's favorite armchair, his foot dangling over the side, and sit like that for hours without saying a word. The only action we'd see out of him was when he'd reach for the fruit bowl. He was always hungry."

When Beverly learned that pot roast was Dean's favorite dish, she arranged to have it whenever he stayed for dinner. They also went on picnics together, or spent the day at the beach, where Jimmy enjoyed racing her small motorboat.

By now Bast's patience with his friend had all but run out. Bills continued to pour in with the speed of an avalanche, and in an effort to keep things going Bast had been borrowing money from whomever he could. "I was losing friends by the gross," he complained.

Perhaps hoping to placate his friend, Dean sometimes invited him along on the frequent outings he and Beverly enjoyed. When Beverly's mother gave her a large party to celebrate her eighteenth birthday, Bast was invited to attend.

The party turned out to be one of the social events of the summer for the Hollywood younger set. Debbie Reynolds, then a promising ingenue at MGM, was there, and so was Lugene Saunders, who was starring in a popular television series.

Bast arrived at the party late from work, feeling tired and out of place among the well-dressed guests.

Dean appeared to be enjoying himself, mingling freely with the others.

A former national archery champion had been hired to entertain, and he was giving a daring exhibition of marksmanship.

Bast sat down alone by the pool, watching as the archer proceeded to break a balloon a volunteer held at arm's length.

The applause no sooner died down than Dean stepped forward, boldly challenging the man to shoot an apple off his head in the manner of William Tell. It was a stunt Miss Davis immediately prohibited as too dangerous.

Dean looked disappointed. Bast's heart sank; for one brief moment he had been hoping the archer might miss his target and nick his friend, nick him only slightly, but nick him just the same.

Several days later the inevitable finally occurred: after another argument over money erupted, Bast decided to move out. He found a room close to the CBS building and gave the landlady a small deposit.

Dean was now on his own, left to enjoy alone the delights of penthouse living, complete with chest-high kitchen sink, Mexican oil portaits, and the rent that went with them.

To Bast's surprise, Dean managed rather well. He borrowed enough money from Beverly to pay some of his bills and began looking for a job, as simple as that.

Through Ted Avery, another disgruntled former usher at CBS, he found a job parking cars on a lot adjacent to the studio. The lot was a haven for out-of-work actors, run by a sympathetic man who

41

allowed his young attendants to take off whenever they needed to go on an interview. The arrangement was ideal for Dean: the CBS executives who used the lot tipped well, bringing his salary almost to that of a full-time job. The hours were good, the work easy, and there was the ever-present chance that a producer or director might discover him.

By now, too, Dean's ability to live off new-found friends was almost a fine art, and before long he was sharing Avery's little Hollywood apartment rent free while the latter's wife was out of town.

An excellent horseman, Avery began teaching Dean how to ride and rope, in the hope Dean could obtain bit parts in cowboy movies as Avery sometimes did. The two of them were frequently seen in the staid corridors of CBS, twirling lariats and cutting up, dressed in full cowboy outfits.

Beverly Wills had moved to Paradise Cove for the rest of the summer to be with her father, and she and Dean saw each other less often. The drive was too far for Dean to make regularly, and moreover he did not get along well with Beverly's new circle of friends, sensing they regarded him as an intruder in their exclusive suburban enclave.

Dean's unpredictability was also becoming upsetting to Beverly. "I learned," she later wrote, "that it was nothing for Jimmy to run through a whole alphabet of emotions in one evening, alternating sharply from low to high and back again, and no one could ever tell what mood would hit him."

At a dance one weekend Dean became jealous when another young man tried to dance with Beverly and almost started a fight. The incident embarrassed Beverly; she and Dean did not see each other for the rest of the summer. This pleased Joan Davis, Beverly's mother. "She couldn't think of any boy who had a less certain future than Jimmy," Beverly said.

Freed from his ties to Beverly, Dean began to spend more time at the CBS studio, trying to cultivate whatever contacts he could. Although nothing came of Avery's plan to get them in Westerns, through another friend Dean was introduced to Ralph Levy, an important TV director at CBS. The so-called "King of Comedies," Levy was directing both the Allan Young and the Ed Wynn shows for the network, and he used Dean as an extra whenever he could.

Levy claimed that even then Dean had a certain presence on stage, a magnetism that more than one person remarked upon. "People in the audience would tell me," the director said, "that when Dean was on stage they found their eyes going to him instead of the star of the show."

Backstage, Levy gave the young actor encouragement and advice, and sometimes during a break in rehearsal the two adjourned to an alley behind the studio to toss around a baseball and talk.

At work on the lot Dean also met a number of producers and directors, but it failed to lead to any acting jobs.

Then one Saturday morning he parked a car for a man named Rogers Brackett. When Dean learned that Brackett directed a weekly CBS program, "Alias Jane Doe," starring Lurene Tuttle, he didn't waste any time confessing he was an actor. Over coffee, the two talked and Brackett casually promised to keep Dean in mind when casting future shows.

True to his word, he soon called Dean in to read

for a small part. Dean's reading was melodramatic and his gestures overly theatrical for a radio studio, but Brackett awarded him the role. It was the first of six shows he did for Brackett. It was also the start of a long and invaluable friendship for Dean, but one that was not without its stormy moments. "I have often thought," Rogers later said, "I should have left 'Hamlet' in the parking lot."

A tall, curly-haired bachelor with good looks and an elegant manner, Brackett was some fifteen years Dean's senior. He was the son of Robert Brackett, an early Hollywood film producer who was once in partnership with Lewis J. Selznick. Born in Culver City, Brackett had literally been raised in Hollywood, and his connections in the film industry were numerous. He himself had served an apprenticeship with David O. Selznick, Lewis' son, and had worked at the Walt Disney Studio. He had left the film business to accept a high-paying position with the advertising firm of Foote, Cone, & Belding as account supervisor. One of his accounts sponsored "Alias Jane Doe," and Brackett doubled as the show's director, an arrangement that was not uncommon.

At this time Brackett was living at the Sunset Plaza, a fashionable apartment house above Sunset Strip.

When Ted Avery's wife returned to Hollywood, Dean was suddenly forced to find another place to live, and he accepted Brackett's invitation to stay with him.

For Dean the Sunset Plaza proved a great improvement over Avery's modest quarters. Built on a hill, it afforded a majestic view of the Valley; Brackett had a comfortable garden apartment which he was subletting from William Goetz, a Universal-International executive. The apartment was adjacent to the swimming pool.

Once again Jimmy had struck it rich—at a friend's expense.

Through Rogers, too, Dean met a large number of people, and there was now glamour and excitement in his life. Rogers took him to private studio screenings, and they would dine at La Rue, a chic restaurant, where Dean liked the Vichyssoise, always pronouncing it "swishy-swashy."

Rogers gave him books to read by writers like Saint-Exupéry and Camus, and Dean absorbed them excitedly, asking for more. "He sapped the minds of his friends," Bast once noted, "like a bloodsucker saps the strength of an unsuspecting man."

But Dean's intelligence was largely intuitive, Brackett felt. Once Dean surprised him by making a mobile, using wire and some chicken bones that had been left over from dinner the night before. When Rogers told him how much he liked the mobile, Dean answered, "What's a mobile?"

Soon Rogers was pretty hung up on his young friend, and they drifted into an affair. "My primary interest in Jimmy was as an actor—his talent was so obvious," Brackett said. "Secondarily, I loved him, and Jimmy loved me. If it was a father-son relationship, it was also somewhat incestuous."

A brilliant stage director, Brackett had had the first Equity company in California, and he began to coach Dean in plays and readings. They rehearsed *Hamlet* on the grand staircase of the Sunset Plaza, overlooking the pool. "Elsinor with room service," Rogers quipped. Then, for contrast, Dean would recite some

45

poems by James Whitcomb Riley he had learned as a boy. " 'Little Orphant Annie' was quite one of his favorites," Brackett remembers. "It was very funny and very touching . . ."

As the war in Korea heated up and Uncle Sam needed soldiers, Dean was called for induction. "Deploring that and any other war," Brackett advised Dean to get out of the draft. "Better the funeral pyre in his Porsche than Korea," Brackett later said. "With his quasi-jock predilections he'd never have made it back . . . I feel."

Through a doctor friend, Brackett set up an appointment with a psychiatrist for Dean. After a viable number of sessions, the shrink came up with a document "that cooled the draft board." When Dean saw Bellah and broke the news of his deferment, he told him, "I kissed the doctor."

Dean's contact with his family had been minimal since leaving UCLA. When he and Rogers visited them in their home in the Valley to pick up some clothes, Dean discovered that to earn extra cash his father was raising chinchillas in a spare bedroom. Rogers thought the scene was something out of *The Day of the Locust*. Conversation was strained all the way around.

Along with David Wayne, the actor, and his wife, Dean and Rogers went to Tijuana for a weekend to see a bullfight, first staying overnight in Laguana. Another time he traveled with Rogers to Mexicali where they saw the matador Arruza in the ring. In Mexicali Dean met Budd Boetticher, a movie director and bullfight aficionado who had served as technical adviser for the film *Blood and Sand*. Boetticher gave Dean a blood-stained cape that had once belonged to

Sidney Franklin, the Brooklyn-bred matador who had achieved fame in the rings of Spain and about whom Hemingway had written.

The cape became Dean's prize possession and thereafter wherever he traveled the cape traveled with him.

Because of Rogers' many friends in the movie business, Jimmy easily found work as an extra. He made his film debut in Paramount's *Sailor Beware*, a Dean Martin-Jerry Lewis comedy. In a boxing sequence Dean acted as a second for Jerry Lewis' opponent. A white towel draped around his neck, Dean spoke his first words on the Silver Screen: "That guy's a professional."

He next appeared in a Korean war movie, *Fixed Bayonets*, starring Richard Basehart, and directed by Samuel Fuller, a friend of Brackett's. Again, Dean had one line of dialogue: "It could be the rear guard coming back." "What a part," he later said.

At Universal-International he had two days' work, playing a teenager in another comedy, *Has Anybody Seen My Gal?*, starring Rock Hudson and Piper Laurie. In the film Dean comes into an ice-cream parlor and orders an elaborate ice cream sundae. The counterman, played by Charles Coburn, asks him to come back the next day for a fitting. Dean described the film as "family-type" entertainment.

It was not until years later when the film was shown on television that Piper Laurie learned she had once made a movie with James Dean.

Not all of Brackett's friends liked Dean, however, or were anxious to advance his career. A meeting Rogers arranged with Leonard Spiegelgass, a story editor at MGM and an important man in the studio hierarchy, ended in disaster when Spiegelgass ordered Dean from his house. "His manners were terrible," Spiegelgass said. "He flicked ashes on the rug and behaved like an animal. The boy was absolute poison." Spiegelgass warned Brackett that he was "ruining his reputation" by pushing Dean so hard, but Brackett paid no attention.

At the Zuma Beach home of George Bradshaw, the short story writer, Dean accidently set fire to one of Bradshaw's favorite armchairs and Brackett had to pay for its repair.

"Jimmy was like a child," Rogers said. "He behaved badly just to get attention."

Like a child, too, Dean seemed to be forever testing the affection of those closest to him. "The only way he could be sure you really loved him," another friend said, "was if you loved him when he was truly at his worst."

By the fall Dean was becoming slightly bored with the life he was leading. He sought out his old friend Bast, whom he had hardly seen since the penthouse fiasco in mid-summer. Bast was now working as a pageboy on several shows at CBS and preparing to start his senior year at UCLA.

"You know," Dean confided to him, "it gets sickening. The other day we were sitting at the pool and I made a bet with Rogers that the names of La Rue or the Mocambo would be dropped at least fifteen times within the next hour. We kept count and I won. What a pile of . . ."

As always, whatever the state of his personal life, Dean's career was foremost in his mind, and he again was worried about his future as an actor. "A guy could go on knocking his brains out, getting nothing but bit parts for years," he told Bast over a bowl of chili at Barney's Beanery. "There's got to be more."

To another struggling actor Dean confessed the same fear. "They'll never give me a real chance out here," he said. "I'm not the bobby-sox type, and I'm not the romantic leading-man type either. Can you imagine me making love to Lana Turner?"

Although he was attending James Whitmore's class less regularly, his respect for the actor remained as great as ever. When Whitmore took him aside after class one evening and spoke to him sharply, Dean listened. "Stop dissipating your energy and talent," Whitmore urged. He told him to "quit just hanging around Hollywood" and go to New York where he would be able to study and master his craft. "Learn to be an actor. It doesn't take anything if all you want to be is just another ham."

If Dean had any lingering doubts about leaving, they were dispelled when Rogers was called to Chicago, the home office of Foote, Cone, & Belding on an important assignment. Eventually, Brackett hoped to be transferred to New York, but he had no idea how many months he might have to remain in Chicago. For the third time in three short months Dean was about to literally lose the roof over his head. It proved to be too much.

"I can't stomach this dung home any more," he told Bast with finality after a late-night talk session.

Several days later, when Bast returned to his apartment after work, he found a message the landlady had left: "Mr. Dean called. Gone to New York."

Chapter 4

Before arriving in New York Jimmy first stopped off in Chicago to see Rogers Brackett, who was staying at the Ambassador East. Brackett remembers Dean made quite a stir striding through the lobby of the expensive hotel dressed in bluejeans and carrying his bullfighter's cape slung over his shoulder. After about a week in the Windy City, Dean visited the Reverend DeWeerd for a few days at his new home in Indianapolis and paid a visit to the farm to see his aunt and uncle. Then he proceeded on his journey.

In New York Dean took a room at the Iroquois Hotel on West 44th Street, several blocks from Times Square.

"New York frightened and overwhelmed me," Dean said afterwards. "For the first few weeks I barely strayed from my hotel. I would see three movies a day to ease the loneliness I felt."

Gradually, as his fears resided, he began to explore the city around him. He took his first subway ride and went on long walks, once wandering as far as South Ferry, near the Battery.

He met a friend, Harry Drake, a young would-be artist who had grown up on a wheat farm in Kansas. The two delved into the big city together, visiting libraries and museums. They searched second-hand bookstores along Eighth Avenue, looking for old bullfight posters, and discovered Hector's, an inexpensive Times Square cafeteria, known for its glazed cakes. Drake was an amateur photographer and Dean sometimes borrowed his equipment and spent the day photographing sights around the city.

In a very real way he was completing his education, learning from all that lay around him. "New York is generous," Dean once said, "and above all fertile . . ."

The money he lived on was largely what he had saved from his work as a movie extra; he had also sold his car before leaving California, but even so now his resources probably amounted to no more than two hundred dollars. When this was nearly gone, Dean got a job washing dishes in a tavern on West 45th Street. To economize he took a small room at the McBurney YMCA on West 63rd Street, just a short block from Central Park.

Before leaving Los Angeles Dean had been given the names of several people to look up, and he now decided to get in touch with them. He called James Sheldon, an advertising executive who was a friend of Ralph Levy's, and made an appointment to see him. He also phoned one of Brackett's friends, Alec Wilder, the composer who had written such popular tunes as "I'll Be Around," and "Who Can I Turn To?" and Wilder invited him over to the Algonquin Hotel, where he then lived. "Rogers had already warned me," Wilder recounts, "to be on the lookout for 'this real wild kid,' but Dean was polite at our initial meeting. I suppose he was so new in town he had to be well behaved."

Dean's first meeting with Sheldon turned out well

too. A big, friendly man then in his late 20's, Sheldon was working as account supervisor at Young & Rubicam, hoping to eventually break into television as a director.

Through his contacts at the agency, he had heard that the young actor who played Nels on the popular TV series "Mama" was about to be drafted into the army, and the network was worried about a replacement. Sheldon thought Dean would be perfect; he had seen the Broadway play *I Remember Mama*, on which the series was based, and Dean reminded him very much of the actor who had played Nels on the stage, a young Midwesterner named Marlon Brando.

Sheldon contacted Doris Quinlan, the show's co-producer, and sent Dean over to read. Miss Quinlan was impressed enough to consider offering Dean a five-year contract, but as things turned out, the would-be soldier failed his army physical and remained on the show.

Still anxious to help, Sheldon then introduced Dean to Jane Deacy, a theatrical agent at the Louis Shurr office. An able and intelligent woman, Miss Deacy had started as a switchboard operator at Shurr and worked her way up, becoming one of the office's top agents. Her clients included Gower Champion, the dancer, and Priscilla Gillette, who had played the lead in *Brigadoon* on Broadway.

To this day, Miss Deacy steadfastly refuses to publicly discuss either her first meeting with Dean or their subsequent relationship. But another employee of the Shurr office recalled: "Jimmy appealed enormously to Jane's maternal instinct. He had that lonely boy quality which women find irresistible. And of course she believed he had talent. Like all good agents she almost has a sixth sense when it comes to finding actors. . . . From the very beginning her faith in Jimmy was utter and complete."

While Miss Deacy set about the task of finding him work, Dean did his best to keep body and soul together on his own.

Through another young actor he found part-time employment on the television game show "Beat the Clock." Dean was paid $5.00 an hour as a stand-in to test lighting and camera angles. He also tried out the show's games during rehearsals, in front of a live audience. Dean liked the work and always showed up for rehearsals on time. Unfortunately, his agility was such that he was able to do stunts that contestants later found impossible, and after a while producer Jean Hollander was forced to find another actor with less coordination.

When winter came, Dean still had not found any steady work as an actor, but his days were far from empty. He avidly followed the trade papers, hoping to come across parts he might audition for. Along with a young actress named Jeanne, whom he had met in the Astor drugstore, a favorite haunt of aspiring actors, Dean informally rehearsed scenes from a wide variety of plays. "He'd phone my apartment at the strangest times," Jeanne remembered, "and ask if it was okay to come by. It might be midnight or four in the afternoon, but when I said yes, he'd come right over, and we'd work together on a scene he had brought."

"Work, study," Whitmore had told him. "Learn to be an actor." In his own way Dean was doing just that.

In January Dean learned that Joan Davis and her daughter Beverly were in town. Miss Davis had come East to do a radio show with Tallulah Bankhead, and she and her daughter were staying at the Plaza. Forgetting the bad feeling of the summer before, Dean phoned Beverly and made a date for dinner.

Beverly was alarmed when she saw Dean: despite the cold he was wearing the same thin blue jacket she remembered from the summer and a pair of dirty gray slacks. In his lapel he had a small matador's sword which he was especially proud of.

They ate in an Italian restaurant, and over dinner Dean sheepishly admitted he had been living largely on milkshakes since leaving Hollywood. Yet, throughout the evening he did his best to maintain an aura of bravado. When he took her back to her hotel and they said good night, Dean promised her, "I'll show them."

Then he left, walking across the park to the little room he had at the Y.

On the other evenings when he was alone Dean often dropped by the Rehearsal Club, looking for companionship. The Club had been built in 1913 to serve as a residence for girls who had come to New York seeking a career in show business. Residents were well chaperoned, and male visitors were only permitted in the lounge until the midnight curfew.

"Jimmy was always hanging around," a former resident said, "whether he had a date or not. The girls at the club all kind of adopted him. One girl I knew even gave him an old camel-hair coat she had worn in college. It was too small on him but he wore it anyway."

One rainy day Dean borrowed an umbrella from a

girl sitting across from him in the lounge. It turned out she was a dancer, named Elizabeth Sheridan, and had been living at the Club several months.

A couple of days later Dean returned her umbrella. She was on her way to a dance rehearsal nearby and Dean went along to watch. "When I first met Jimmy," she later said, "he looked like a straggly, hungry kid who needed a friend. After, I found he always looked that way."

Of mixed Irish-Jewish ancestry, Dizzy, as everyone called her, was the daughter of Frank Sheridan, the classical pianist, and had grown up in Westchester. Another friend at the time described her as "a long, lithe, supple beauty with a pixie humor that came across in everything she said and did."

Like Dean, she had left school against her family's wishes to pursue her career, and like Dean she was very broke.

"We would sit and talk for hours and hours," Dizzy remembers, "getting to know each other better all the time." Sometimes Dean would call and play records for her over the phone. "It was a desperate feeling we had toward needing each other," Dizzy said, "and pretty soon we got to be inseparable."

They spent much of their time at Jerry's, a small Italian place on 54th Street, not far from the Rehearsal Club. There was a new drink called Champale they both liked, and the restaurant's proprietor, Jerry Lucce, allowed them to stay as long as they wanted over a single bottle.

"Lots of times," Dizzy remembers, "we used to walk along Fifth Avenue and look in store windows. Mostly it was cars. He was fascinated by cars. He always wanted a Jaguar and I always wanted a Jaguar and there was a place on Broadway up around the Sixties, a great big store window that had all sorts of cars in it. We used to hang around and look in the window and dream about the Jaguar we were someday going to get. It turned out he got a Porsche, or it got him."

Dean's faith in himself remained firm as ever. "He never for one instant doubted he would make it," Dizzy claimed. "I mean he always knew that he would one day be a star, and there was no question in his mind about it at all."

When she and Dean finally realized how much time they were spending in each other's company, they decided it would probably be just as easy to move in together. They found a room at the Hargrave Hotel on West 72nd Street, off Columbus Avenue. Their room was the size of a broom closet, Dizzy recalled, and the wallpaper was peeling off in layers. But they hung up a few drawings Dean had done in his sketchbook and called the place home.

Dean brought along a hotplate he had used to cook on at the Y, and he and Dizzy prepared simple meals on it. "He was always talking about steaks," Dizzy said. "How he loved good steaks . . . but in the early part of our relationship we didn't do much eating."

To avoid buying any new clothes they wore each other's spare bluejeans. On cold nights when the old radiator broke down, Dean's bullfighter's cape served as an extra blanket to keep them warm.

Jimmy taught Dizzy to sketch, telling her to look out the window and draw what she saw. One morning Dean had an early appointment with a casting agent, but before he left, he made a hardboiled egg and left it on a table for Dizzy when she awoke. He drew a face on the egg and wrote a cheerful note.

"What I remember most about Jimmy was his gentleness," recalls Dizzy, a stage actress today and married to a composer. "Ours was a very private relationship. During the time we were together we saw as few other people as possible. It was the way both of us wanted it."

Early in February Dean turned 21. He and Dizzy celebrated at Jerry's, along with a few friends of hers from the Rehearsal Club. Dean told her it was the "best birthday he had had in years."

A week later, Dean received a fitting if belated birthday present. Archer King, a young agent at the Shurr Office who worked closely with Jane Deacy, sent him to read for a part on "The Web," a half-hour mystery program. The role was that of a bellhop who helps solve a murder at a plush mountain resort. "The minute he started reading," said Lela Swift, the director, "I knew that boy had something special."

Along with Anne Jackson, E.G. Marshall, and Robert Simon, Dean was cast in the show.

As soon as rehearsals began, however, Dean's temperament got him in trouble. Producer Franklin Heller found him "unresponsive to suggestions," "very difficult," "not on time," and "generally a pain in the ass." Had it not been for Miss Swift, who insisted on having him in the part, Dean probably would have been fired.

After a four-day rehearsal the show was done live on February 20th, a Wednesday. Even those who had been most skeptical were impressed by Dean's performance. "He gave us all a terrible time in rehearsal," Anne Jackson commented, "but on the air he was just marvelous." Franklin Heller went out of his way to tell Dean how good he had been. Dean murmured his thanks. "He was as gracious," Heller said later, "as Jimmy Dean could be."

Following his success, Dean was quickly signed to appear on another television show, "Martin Kane," a private eye series. Once again, rehearsals had no sooner started than Dean was at odds with the rest of the cast, and this time with the show's director, Frank Burns, as well.

"Dean was a very inventive actor," explained Edgar Kahn, another director at the studio. "But in those days television shows were 'shot tight.' The emphasis was on getting the job done as quickly and cheaply as possible. There wasn't enough time for the constant probing of a part Dean liked."

After several warnings, Dean was fired by director Burns; the show had been in rehearsal two days.

When Dean returned to the Shurr office and Archer King asked for an explanation, Dean told him curtly: "I was trying to get a characterization. I couldn't worry about going to some damn chalk mark."

His television career temporarily sidetracked, Dean turned to Dizzy, relying on her to get him through the blue periods he often fell prey to.

Since their hotel was close to Central Park, they would go there in the afternoons when the weather was mild. Dean liked to take along his sketchbook and bullfighter's cape. To take his mind off everything, he practiced his capework by the hour while Dizzy watched, or sketched, or read, his audience of one.

When their money finally ran out, Dizzy went to work as a retoucher for the American Photograph Corporation, and Dean took whatever jobs he could.

He worked as an extra on "Tales of Tomorrow," a science fiction show, and landed a bit part on Studio One. Once again Dean played a bellhop. The show, "10,000 Horses Singing," starred John Forsythe.

During this time, Dean grew closer to Jane Deacy, his agent, visiting her Yorkville apartment where she lived with her husband, a radio engineer, and their young son. Miss Deacy would slip Dean five dollars or so, telling him when he became a star he could pay her back. Dean now called her "Mom."

Dean also introduced Dizzy to Alec Wilder, and Wilder liked her at once. "She was a wonderful girl," Wilder said, "and an extremely good influence for Dean. He needed her. Whenever she was with him, he was calmer and more stable than usual."

Toward the end of the winter Dizzy took Jimmy to Larchmont to meet her family, and then the two of them drove to Connecticut for a day, visiting Daycroft, Dizzy's old school.

In late March their funds ran out again, and they were forced to move out of their hotel. Dizzy found a tiny room on Eighth Avenue, and Dean went to live with Rogers Brackett, who had come to New York several months earlier. Still working for Foote, Cone & Belding, Brackett was now with their Madison Avenue office and had a loft apartment on West 38th Street, just off Fifth Avenue.

As in the past, Brackett was only too glad to help his young protege. One of the accounts he handled was the Hallmark Company, which sponsored the Hallmark Hall of Fame, and by pulling a few strings he got them to hire Dean.

For his paycheck each week Dean was required to

do little more than show up at the studio; the only actual duty he had was to stand at a blackboard and list the show's credits as the program went off the air. This was done live and in close-up, showing only Dean's hand on camera. But even to this Jimmy was able to bring a flair that was all his own: invariably as he got to the final words "devised and directed by Albert McCleery," he would either break the chalk or scrape it in such a way as to make an unpleasant noise.

Albert McCleery was never sure whether this was accidental or not, but because of Brackett he was forced to put up with Dean anyway.

For Dean life now seemed curiously happy. He and Dizzy were still together much of the time, but there were again gay times with Rogers too: evenings spent at the ballet or dining in expensive restaurants.

On Sunday nights, after the Hallmark telecast, Sarah Churchill, the show's hostess, held open house for the cast at her penthouse on Central Park South, and Dean and Brackett always went. To entertain her guests Miss Churchill did imitations of her father, Sir Winston, and told amusing stories of what it had been like being the Prime Minister's daughter.

Dean seemed almost star-struck by these gatherings, and was fond of Miss Churchill, who would take him aside and lecture him good-naturedly about his behavior, especially the tricks he played on Albert McCleery.

As if to underscore his present good fortune, Dean got a lead on the "U.S. Steel Radio Hour," playing a friend of young Abe Lincoln in "Prologue to Glory." He worked with John Lund and Wanda Hendrix, both already well established actors.

All in all, it was not a bad way for an Indiana farm boy to mark his first six months in New York City.

Then, as winter finally ended and spring filled the air, Dean heard some more good news: another old friend was coming to New York.

William Bast had written, saying that as soon as he graduated, he planned to come East to live, and he promised to look Dean up the very moment he got to town.

Chapter 5

During Bast's first week in New York, Dean gave him what amounted to an orientation program. He took him on his acting rounds, showed him the sights of the city, and introduced him to people.

Bast was struck by the poise and sense of self-assurance Dean had acquired; no longer was he the frightened young man, unsure of his future, that Bast remembered. He now seemed confident and more determined, and Bast could feel it.

"I've discovered a whole new world here," Dean told him. "A whole new way of thinking . . . this town's the end. It's talent that counts here. You've got to stay with it or get lost. I like it."

Because of his past experiences, Bast easily found a job with CBS, working in the communications department. He had already given up the idea of becoming an actor, and instead hoped to write, either novels or short stories. Until he became more firmly settled, he took a room at the Iroquois.

Dizzy was offered a job in stock in Ocean City, New Jersey, as an assistant choreographer, and decided to take it. Dean left Brackett's apartment and moved in with Bast.

Jimmy now decided to do something he had long

planned on: audition for the Actors Studio, the famed workshop conducted by Lee Strasberg and Elia Kazan. Dean had first heard of the school through James Whitmore, who encouraged him to seek admittance, but until now he had not felt he was ready.

For his audition Dean decided to team up with Christine White, a young actress who also was a client of Jane Deacy's.

Blond and petite, Chris was from Washington, D.C., and had studied English literature at the University of North Carolina. She was then sharing a cramped apartment on 92nd Street and Madison Avenue with several college friends.

Before coming to New York Chris had acted in stock on Cape Cod and had arrived in the city only a few weeks earlier. She had come by sea plane, a fact that intrigued Dean immediately.

"Jimmy was an impulsive, immediate creature," remembers Chris, who later won acclaim in *A Hat Full of Rain* on Broadway. "He could look at a delicatessen window and suddenly start waving at a bowl of prunes like they were alive. He was childish in a charming way."

The scene they chose was one that Chris had written. It ran for seven pages and involved an encounter on a beach between an intellectual drifter and an aristocratic Southern girl.

In order to get the proper outdoors feeling, Dean insisted they rehearse in the open, either in Central Park or on the sunroof of Chris's apartment building.

Over a period of several weeks they shaped and molded the scene. They tried it out in front of Bast and Chris's roommates, and to get the reaction of others Jimmy would stop strangers in the park and ask them to watch.

Despite their preparation, on audition day Dean was understandably nervous. They had brought along a bottle of beer as a prop for the scene, but in his excitement Dean drank the bottle and had to run out for another.

Finally their turn came. As the scene opened, Dean was supposed to be gazing at the stars, speculating about a coming hurricane. "Well," Chris remembers, "Jimmy couldn't see a thing without his glasses. He couldn't even find center stage. And he couldn't even find me when I made my entrance. But every line came out clear."

Usually studio auditions are limited to five minutes, at the end of which the judges ring a bell. But when Chris and Dean ran several minutes over the allotted time they were not interrupted.

Out of the 150 who auditioned only 15 were accepted; both Dean and Christine White were among them. At 21 Dean was one of the youngest members ever to be admitted.

That night he elatedly took Chris to Jerry's for dinner, and, as an encore, they did the scene for Jerry Lucce.

Encouraged by his achievement, Dean got to work at once on his first studio project.

He had recently read and liked a novel by Barnaby Conrad, *Matador*, and decided to dramatize a chapter from it. The book is about an aging matador whose pride forces him to accept a challenge from a young rival, even though it means almost certain death.

Dean wanted to convey the man's emotions as he prepares for the final flight. The acting was to be an internal monologue, done without words, and using only a few props: a statue of the Virgin, a candle, and the matador cape.

Once again Dean worked hard to get his work ready. "When he prepared an acting job," Bast said, "he put his heart and soul into it."

The performance was done in front of a full session of the Studio, presided over by Lee Strasberg.

A small, catlike man, Strasberg was then already a living legend, known as the founder of the so-called Method school of acting, based on the theories of the Russian director, Constantin Stanislavski. According to the Method, actors were encouraged to draw on their own past experiences to project themselves emotionally in a role.

As a teacher, Strasberg's criticisms were often sharp and abrasive, his manner rather formal. Students called him "The Archbishop." Some at the Studio compared his technique of taking apart an actor's performance to that of a surgeon cutting away bad tissue; others said the whole process was more like being raked over hot coals.

Always sensitive to criticism, Dean was not ready for the strong critique Strasberg launched into. As Chris White recalled, "Jimmy's face turned ashen," and when Strasberg finished speaking, Dean simply threw his bullfight cape over his shoulder and walked out without saying a word.

The experience had shaken him deeply.

"I don't know what's inside of me," he told Bill Bast. "I don't know what happens when I act . . . But if I let them dissect me like a rabbit in a laboratory I might not be able to produce again.

"That man had no right to tear me down like that.

65

You keep knocking a guy down like that and you take the guts away from him. And what's an actor without guts?"

Angered and hurt, for a long time Dean swore he would never return to the Studio.

As summer crept upon the city, so did the annual show business hiatus, the time when television programs went off the air and theaters closed their doors, leaving actors to sweat out the muggy New York summer.

In July the Hallmark show suspended its programing until the fall, and Dean's sinecure came to an abrupt end.

"Like a variation on an old theme," Bast wrote, "money soon became a major problem again. It was a common occurrence for us to divide the 60 or 70 cents we might have between us to buy a slim dinner at the Automat." Lunch, he added, became a "forgotten social pastime."

At loose ends, with no prospect of work in sight, Jimmy seemed unable to orient himself. He drifted along, sleeping late, rarely leaving his hotel room before noon, and then not to go very far. He would sit for hours on the steps of the hotel barber shop, until Louis, the proprietor, chased him for blocking the entrance. Alec Wilder, who lived down the block at the Algonquin, recalled, "I don't know how many hundreds of times I'd come into the lobby and find Dean sprawled on the bellboys' bench."

One weekend Dizzy came into town for a visit. *Has Anybody Seen My Gal?*, the movie Dean did the summer before, had opened at the Mayfair Theater, and he, Dizzy, and Bast went to see it. When Dean came on screen, the three of them stood up and cheered. Dizzy convinced Dean to return to Ocean City with her, feeling the change might do him good. Dean went, but after several days of hanging around the sleepy seaside resort he grew restless and was anxious to return to New York and again try for work.

He auditioned without success for a lead in a forthcoming television series, "Life with Father," based on Clarence Day's best-selling book. He also tried to land the part of Curly in *Oklahoma!*, which Mike Todd was planning to bring to the screen. At the casting office Dean met a young actor named Paul Newman, whom he had seen at other auditions. "We were like the Bobbsey Twins," Newman claimed. "Every place I went, he went." But, like Dean, Newman was not signed for the Todd movie either.

In August, as summer reached its peak and the city turned into a drab desert of concrete, another opportunity shimmered on the horizon, like an oasis, and with that strange combination of luck and guile that had propelled him through life thus far, Dean was quick to reach for it.

He was offered a job as a deckhand aboard a yacht chartered by Lemuel Ayers, a friend of Rogers Brackett's. A charming and talented Princeton graduate, Ayers was a well-known set designer and had coproduced Cole Porter's *Kiss Me Kate*. He was then preparing a new play for Broadway, *See the Jaguar*, by N. Richard Nash.

Ayers lived with his wife and two children in an old Victorian house near Nyack, New York, in Rockland County. Brackett and Dean sometimes spent weekends there, where Jimmy enjoyed himself entertaining Ayers' young children, Sarah and Jonathan.

Although Brackett had already suggested Dean for a part in Ayers' new play, the producer felt he lacked experience. But the job as deckhand was open.

Dean joined the crew and the sloop sailed for Martha's Vineyard. Aboard were Ayers, his wife Shirley, and several guests. The trip lasted almost two weeks; the first day out the weather was bad and the sea turned rough. When the sloop reached New London, several people, including Alec Wilder, decided to get off and return by train. But Dean stayed, enjoying himself, quickly learning about lines and spars, sheets and shrouds—a farmboy turned deckhand. A young Gatsby in the making.

By the time the sloop returned to port, Ayers had been impressed enough by Dean to reconsider his earlier decision. He promised that when *See the Jaguar* was cast, Dean would be given a reading. But whether he got the part would depend on how well he did.

Before Dean left for the trip, he and Bast had decided to give up their hotel room. Apparently unconcerned about where he would live when he returned—after all, Bast claimed, it "was a whole ten days off"—Dean left the problem of finding new quarters to his friend.

Bast found a temporary solution by moving in with an old girl friend from UCLA, and Jimmy joined them. Shortly after Labor Day, however, the girl's lease was up and they were all forced to move again. Along with Dizzy, who had returned to the city and was now working as an usherette at the Paris Theater, they found a small apartment at 13 West 89th Street in an old Brownstone right off Central Park.

The new apartment proved something of an adventure at first. A brick street ran in front of the building, and every evening they could hear the sound of horses' hoofs as the police cavalry returned to the stables down the block. The whole atmosphere, Bast wrote, suggested a quainter era, as though they were all back in the days of hansom cabs and horseless carriages, and Lillian Russell and Diamond Jim Brady were the talk of the town.

As the weeks rolled by, Dean kept in touch with Ayers' office, checking on the show's progress. Each time he called, though, Dean's disappointment grew: plans were lagging; problems had arisen that no one had counted on.

From Brackett Dean learned the producer was having problems rounding up potential backers. *See the Jaguar* was his first dramatic venture, and investors were wary. Furthermore, there were difficulties casting the show's leads. One actor was waiting to see if he might be signed for Arthur Miller's *The Crucible* before committing himself to Ayers.

Privately Brackett wondered if the show would get off the ground, but he urged Dean to be patient.

At this time, too, Dean's newest living arrangements were proving less than perfect. "After the novelty wore off," Bast wrote, "community living ceased to be an adventure and became a problem . . . If we weren't battling over the maze of bras, panties, and stockings that were making access to the bathroom impossible, we were haggling over the unwashed dishes . . . the selection of radio programs, etc., etc."

One evening after a skimpy meal of chili and beans,

Dean announced he was going home to Indiana for a couple of weeks. He was tired of the delays on the show and wanted time to think about his future. He invited the others to go along. "We'll hitchhike out there," he told them. "It's only 800 miles." Dizzy accepted at once, and after some persuasion Bast decided to make the trip too. Toni, their other roommate, promised to phone CBS every day and tell them Bast was sick.

With ten dollars to sustain them, and one battered suitcase, the three took a bus the next morning to the New Jersey Turnpike and started hitchhiking.

By nightfall they found themselves still in Pennsylvania, weary and hungry, and a long way from Fairmount. After having ice cream at a small roadside place, they got a ride with a man driving an old Nash Rambler. His name was Clyde McCullough and he was a catcher for the Pittsburgh Pirates. He was on his way to Des Moines, Iowa, to play a game with a team that was barnstorming across the country.

When they stopped for coffee and McCullough, who is today a catching instructor in the New York Mets organization, discovered his companions had hardly eaten, he insisted on buying them dinner.

They drove with him the rest of the way to Indiana, passing the cold night singing and telling stories, Jimmy and Dizzy huddled in the back seat to keep warm.

Just before dawn, they reached Fairmount, and parted on the highway, all good friends.

On the farm the three quickly entered into a new tempo and pace of life. They were up and about bright and early. Dean taught Dizzy how to shoot a rifle, using tin cans as targets. At the first opportunity Dean got his old motorcycle out of the workshed and put on a daring exhibit of stunt riding. "I'll never sell it," he told Bast. "It's like a friend and brother to me. And friends are hard to find in the theater."

The Winslows were glad to have Jimmy home and made his two friends feel welcome. There were clean, warm beds and plenty to eat, and every night after supper everyone sat around talking.

"After all the years of seeing Jimmy alone and without a family," Bast commented, "it was a wonderful thing to watch him touch again the gentle roots of his early years. He was back in his element again and he loved it."

"Someday when I make it," Dean vowed, "I'm going to see to it that they sell this place and move to a drier climate where Mom's arthritis won't bother her so much. Some day they're going to have the kind of life they deserve, without all the work and worry."

Dean revisited his old high school and took Bast and Dizzy around town, showing them his former boyhood haunts. He and Dizzy also went horseback riding, enjoying the Indiana countryside that had turned golden now in the early autumn. "I wish everybody could have been with us in Indiana," Dizzy later said, "and seen how good and simple Jimmy really was. I can remember his love for animals, how close he could get to them, and even the tender way he treated the soil around the farm."

After a week there was an unexpected phone call from New York. It was Lemuel Ayers' office, telling Dean *Jaguar* was finally set to go into production and they wanted him to audition.

The next morning, Dean and his two friends were

driven by Uncle Marcus to the main highway and started to thumb their way back.

All were silent and sorry to be leaving, but at least luck was with them: the first driver who stopped turned out to be going to New York. He was a wealthy oilman from Texas, and he suffered from ulcers. Every time they stopped for something to eat he would go outside and become violently ill. Finally Dean took the wheel, and as night fell, drove toward the city.

Chapter 6

Back in New York Jimmy prepared for his audition.

"He had had a dream in the back of his mind all these months," Bast said, "and he was determined to make that dream come true."

On the night of his reading, dressed in a clean shirt he had borrowed from Bast and a pair of newly pressed slacks, Dean showed up at Ayers' office on West 57th. He was reading for the part of Wally Wilkins, a backward youth who finds himself at the mercy of a sadistic mountain community.

The part had been an extraordinarily difficult one to cast; over a hundred young actors had already been interviewed, including several in Hollywood and Chicago, and almost forty were invited to audition. "While we'd been considering some of the more promising ones," the director, Michael Gordon, remembers, "we'd found none who wholly satisfied us."

Gordon was alone in Ayers' office when Dean arrived. "I was instantly alerted to what seemed to me an exciting potential for the role," Gordon recalls. "He was young enough, off-beat enough, and still appealing enough to bring to the character the mixture of qualities the role called for. The question was, could he act?"

Gordon handed Dean a script and indicated one or two scenes he wanted him to read. Dean sat in the outer office studying the script for almost an hour. Then he and Gordon started going over the first scene. "It was only a matter of minutes until I knew that he was what I'd been searching and hoping for," Gordon said. "His impulses and criteria were right on the beam."

At 21 Dean was cast in his first Broadway play. He joined Arthur Kennedy and Constance Ford, who had already been selected for the two leads. Others in the cast included Roy Fant, Margaret Barker, George Tyne, David Clarke, Florence Sundstrom, and Cameron Prud'homme.

Rehearsals got underway on October 20th, and Jimmy was soon right at home on Broadway, plastering his dressing room with bullfight posters and picture postcards of toreros he admired. "He claimed, among other things," the director remembers, "to have been a novillero in various bullrings south of the border, and I often saw him make daring passes and farinas at onrushing taxicabs while crossing Broadway or Seventh Avenue."

For Dean, things went exceedingly well, and he got on smoothly with the others.

"He was a prince," Constance Ford said, "and the first time I saw him I knew it." Originally, Nash had wanted Maureen Stapleton for the lead, but the part went to Miss Ford, a television actress and former Conover model, after the other actress turned it down. At the playwright's suggestion Constance had dyed her hair brunette for the part. When Dean

74

wandered into her dressing room and saw her studying her new hair color, he told her: "It doesn't make you Maureen Stapleton." They became good friends.

In the show Dean played a young man who has spent most of his life in an icehouse, hidden away from the world by his half-demented mother. Upon her death, he emerges outside, only to be caged by a cruel storekeeper to whom his mother owed money. To get a feeling of what it was like to be penned in, Dean even locked himself in a closet and stayed there overnight. "His intuitive impulses were beautiful and he had the courage as an actor to go with them," Gordon said. "I never saw him do a better job on TV or film that I felt surpassed the work he did in *See the Jaguar*."

As rehearsals progressed, however, it became clear the show was headed for difficulties.

The play was under-capitalized, and to save money on an orchestra, Alec Wilder, who had been signed to write background music, was forced to write a score using only choral voices that could be put on tape.

Several actors thought the script was too ambiguous and that there was no rationale for the brutal behavior of the characters they portrayed. One actor, Tony Krabner, felt the play was a subtle warning against domestic Fascism, with the mountain hamlet representing a microcosm of the country as a whole. As things turned out, that interpretation proved as good as any.

The play opened out of town for a week-long run at the Parson's Theater in New Haven, Connecticut, before moving on to Philadelphia for a two-week engagement at the Forrest Theater.

In Philadelphia notices in both the local papers were good and morale improved. Dean managed to enjoy himself. He and his understudy, Dane Knell, met some girls from another show who were staying at their hotel, and each night after the play they went on the town, staying out until the early morning hours.

On December 3, 1952, *See the Jaguar* opened at the Cort Theater on Broadway.

"We knew it was a flop opening night," Alec Wilder said. In the first act, the stereo equipment on which Wilder's music had been recorded broke down, and no one was able to fix it. In the second, the stage manager missed a prop cue and neglected to shoot a gun, marring a crucial scene. At the end of the act, Arthur Kennedy came off stage and said quietly, "Well, that's it."

At the traditional opening party at Sardi's the cast and their friends waited for the morning papers and the critics' reactions.

Ayers and his wife tried their best to remain optimistic. The room was filled with people, and there was a great deal of noise and laughter. One actress said afterwards, "It was the nicest dirge I've ever been to."

Dean had invited Bast and Dizzy and the three of them sat at a small table in the corner. Dean was ecstatic; his own dressing room had been jammed with well-wishers after the show and compliments about his performance had filled the air.

Every once in a while Dean excused himself and went off to mingle with the others. As Dizzy and Bast watched him bounce around the room, accepting congratulations or posing with his proud agent, they felt strangely depressed. They sensed the good times they all had had together were forever at an end, and their old friend Jimmy was on his way, this time alone.

As expected, *See the Jaguar* received an unfavorable press. Brooks Atkinson, writing in *The New York Times*, called the production "a mess." Another critic claimed the play was "obscure," and in the *Daily News* John Chapman's review was headlined, "See the Jaguar Lovely to See and Hear, but It Makes No Sense."

Despite the hostile tone of the reviews, several critics singled Dean out for a brief word of praise. William Hawkins in the *World-Telegram & Sun* wrote, "James Dean is gently awkward as the ignorant boy." John Chapman called Dean's acting "very good," and Walter Kerr, the respected critic for the *Herald Tribune*, stated, "James Dean adds an extraordinary performance in an almost impossible role."

The play closed December 6 after five performances. But Dean had been noticed, and indeed he was on his way.

1953 began auspiciously. In January Dean appeared in a brief dramatic segment on the Kate Smith Variety Show, and also had a role on NBC's "T-Men in Action." Dean played the son of a moonshiner whose mountain still is raided by Treasury agents.

Jane Deacy had left the Schurr office in August to start her own agency and had taken Dean with her. He soon became her hottest client. Job offers came in steadily, but Miss Deacy was careful to pick and choose: there were to be no more walk-ons, no more bits, no more playing bellhops.

In the beginning of February Dean appeared on "You Are There," a popular TV series which recreated historical events. The episode was "The Capture of Jesse James" and Dean played Bob Ford, the man who "shot poor Jesse in the back." Jimmy considered it his "juiciest" role to date. "He loved the part," Sidney Lumet, the director, remembers, "loved handling guns, and used to practice 'quick draw' with all the pleasure of a child." Afterwards, Dean would frequently tell friends it was his dream to make a "great Western."

With the money he was now earning, Dean permitted himself a few small luxuries. He bought a second-hand Leica camera and learned to operate it. He also purchased a glorious tome on bullfighting written in Spanish, José Cossio's *Los Toros*.

Since he could now afford a place of his own, Dean moved out of the apartment he had shared with the others and took a room at the Iroquois Hotel. He and his old friends began to see less of each other, as they had expected, until they all drifted their separate ways. Dizzy was offered a job with a dancing troupe in the West Indies and moved to St. Thomas to live. Bast left for Hollywood, hoping to write scripts for a television show that was going into production. Before he left, Dean told him: "Remember . . . don't take any of their guff out there."

Dean began to spend a good deal of time alone now, studying, learning, seeking out new experiences. "An actor must have a cardinal interest in all things," he liked to say. "To interpret life you must study every aspect of it."

Music interested him so he bought a recorder, an English flutelike instrument, and learned to play it, practicing in his room the simple tunes Alec Wilder would write.

He studied Roman history and dabbled in hypnosis. He tried the parachute jump at Coney Island and attended Christian Science lectures—all just for the experience.

He walked the city streets, stopping to talk to anyone who looked interesting, anyone he might learn from: shoeshine boys, newsstand operators, policemen. He became acquainted with short-order cooks, artists, and even a blind beggar named "Moondog" who dressed in flowing robes and made music using dried bones.

A cab driver, Arnie Langer, claimed: "Dean was always studying working people like me. When I finally saw him on TV, I realized he used me in some of his acting and he used other people I knew too."

Actress Jean Alexander remembers once seeing Dean stand outside a restaurant for twenty minutes, just looking through the window at people while they ate; another actress, Arlene Sachs, who met Dean at the Museum of Modern Art and whom he dated, later said: "When I was in a room with him, I always had the feeling I should open the window and say, 'Fly, Bird.' "

It seemed anything interested him. "I think the prime reason for existence, for living in this world is discovery," he would tell people. There is a story that he once watched a parrot in a cage for a full hour, fascinated by the bird's behavior. There is another story that a month before his death Dean met a plumber and questioned the man incessantly, wanting to know everything about pipes and valves and the working of toilets.

Some who knew the actor claim this insatiable curiosity amounted to a foreknowledge that he did not have long to live, and that he wanted to utilize whatever time he had. Others feel differently. "He loved life so painfully," Arlene Sachs believed, "he wanted to explore everything."

Sometimes Dean liked to boast, "Even if I live to be a hundred I'll never do all the things I want to do." But at other times he would sound fatalistic, too. "I'll never make it to the age of thirty," he confided to more than one friend.

In any event, Dean's life in New York was rich and full; new friends supplanted the old, his circle of acquaintances grew. There was very little lull between acting jobs, and now when he appeared on television, it was his name which frequently headed the cast list. He was not yet a star, but it was a portent of things to come.

A week after one such show in which he had the lead, Dean went into a department store to purchase some undergarments. The friend who was with him remembered the clerk at the counter became deferential after recognizing Dean, but Dean was brusque and rude. "The last time I was in this store," he explained arrogantly, "nobody paid any attention to me. I was too small. All of a sudden I guess I've grown a few inches."

Alas, this also was a portent of things to come.

Chapter 7

In the spring of 1953 MGM offered to fly Dean to Hollywood for a screen test. On the advice of Jane Deacy, Dean turned the offer down. Miss Deacy felt that her client was not yet ready for films, and his TV career was going well enough so that he could wait.

Hollywood would beckon again, she assured him, and the next time their offer would have to be a better one.

In a single week in April, Dean had the lead on two separate television shows. In the first, he played a safecracker; two days later he appeared as a "reform school graduate" named Arbie Ferris on "T-Men in Action." The show was sandwiched in between "Amos & Andy" and a Yankee-Senators baseball game; another young actor named Ben Gazzara was also in the cast.

The program notes state simply: "Arbie learned the hard way, almost too late, that crime does not pay."

But Dean was learning crime did pay—or playing criminals did anyway. Usually he commanded between $200 and $300 for a show, which was not bad, considering it only involved four or five days' work, including rehearsals.

As Dean had almost no head for money, Miss Deacy wisely held on to all his earnings, and he lived off an allowance she gave him. Whenever he wanted something extra, he had to ask her. Reluctantly she permitted him to have a motorcycle, and Dean bought an Indian 550, a sleek machine he dashed around the city on, often with a pretty girl seated behind him.

He now moved out of his hotel, too, first subletting an apartment on West 56th Street from an airline pilot, and then taking a small flat of his own on the top floor of a brownstone at 19 West 68th Street. Right off Central Park, the building was in a neighborhood Dean could rightly call his old one.

The apartment soon became a gathering place for other young actors. "The same people were always there," someone said, "and nobody ever wanted to go home." The regulars included Marty Landau, a friend from Dean's days on "Beat the Clock," and Bill Gunn, a young Negro who introduced Dean to the bongo drums.

But Dean himself moved in many different worlds and various milieus; he seldom introduced his friends to each other and each one knew him as something different. "He had a vital gift for bringing people into their own focus," said Rusty Slocum, then a young actor. "When you were with Jimmy, he could make you feel like you were the one person in his life."

Girls moved in and out of his life in rapid succession; friends soon lost count of them. He would meet a girl at Walgreen's or Cromwell's drugstore in the morning, and by the evening she would be replaced by someone else.

Some lingered longer. He went out with Betsy

Palmer and spent a good deal of time with Arlene Sachs. "He could make a moment," Arlene said. "Just walking down the street with him was like an adventure."

Betsy thought Dean was basically disinterested in the sex act. But Arlene has different recollections: "He was an Aquarius and I'm an Aries," she said, "and the two of us really got it on together."

Intellectually this was an exciting time for Jimmy too. He read Kafka and T.E. Lawrence, Hemingway's *Death in the Afternoon*, and even *I Go Pogo*. He hung out in Greenwich Village at places like Minetta's and the San Remo, and went to film showings at art houses, seeing the movies of Gerard Philipe and Harry Bauer. "Anyone who hasn't seen Harry Bauer," Dean said, "doesn't know what movie art can be."

But Dean never lost track of his primary purpose— to grow as an actor. "His appetite for life was enormous," a friend said, "but acting was his place in this world."

As a change from the criminals he was playing on television, Dean sought other roles. Jane Bowles wanted him for the lead in her play *In the Summer House*, but producer Oliver Smith thought he wasn't right for the part. Through Frank Corsaro, however, Dean landed a small part in an off-Broadway production of *The Scarecrow*. The show opened at the Theater DeLys June 16, 1953 for a limited two-week engagement, and Dean appeared in the cast along with Eli Wallach, William Redfield, and Patricia Neal.

At Corsaro's suggestion Dean also did something he swore he would never do: he made peace with Lee Strasberg and returned to the Actors Studio.

The peace was never more than an uneasy one.

"Jimmy was always talking about the Studio," remembers Claire Heller. "One minute he'd say how terrific it was. Then the next minute he'd tell you the whole thing was a lot of crap. He was very changeable."

Dean appeared as the cadet Starkson in the original studio production of *End as a Man*, and played Pierrot in a production of Edna St. Vincent Millay's *Aria Da Capo*. Director Fred Stewart wanted to do the play in public, but Miss Millay's sister Norma, her literary executrix, considered the production too avant-garde.

Dean also did a scene from Chekov's *The Sea Gull* with Joseph Anthony, who later directed *The Rainmaker* on Broadway. Dean played Treplev, and according to Anthony, "Dean totally identified with the character, a fellow wanting to be a writer, on the outs with society, and in trouble with his family." To think himself into the role, Dean told Anthony he pretended Stella Adler was his mother. Strasberg said afterwards he thought the scene was "lovely."

As Dean's reputation as an actor grew, so did his reputation as a personality. Within New York acting circles he was now known as something of a character, an eccentric. Ever since his school days in Fairmount Dean had stood out from the others, and now in the most diverse city in the world he continued to do so. It was no small feat.

Sometimes he might drop by a friend's apartment, say hello, take food from the refrigerator, eat, and then depart without saying another word. At photographer Roy Schatt's apartment Dean once took a chair and sat in the street on it, disregarding the traffic. Another time, Schatt recalls, Dean somehow wound up standing in the nude on the sidewalk. "He was a mess," Schatt said. Their friendship later ended in an argument.

Dean would go days without shaving and carried around a revolver with one bullet in it. He bought a porkpie hat and wore it indoors and out until he tired of it. One friend remembers waiting for Dean in a hotel lobby and having him show up dressed in a dyed black trenchcoat, wearing a Swedish candle ring on his head. He had just bought the ornament in a thrift shop, he explained.

This was in an era when even actors were expected to dress conventionally. "You were supposed to respect your craft," Richard Grayson explains. "If you showed up at a casting office without a jacket and tie they might not let you audition."

But Jimmy dressed as he pleased, and acted as he pleased.

At an interview with casting agent Marion Daugherty, Dean went to sleep and had to be revived with coffee. His chronic lateness drove directors and fellow actors crazy. Once he missed a dress rehearsal entirely; he was sitting alone in a coffee shop and forgot about it.

After a meeting with Dean, producer Lawrence Langner drew a caricature of him and hung it on his office wall. He labeled it "a commentary on the sad state of the modern actor." The drawing looks remarkably like one of Saint-Exupéry's illustrations for *The Little Prince*, Dean's favorite book, the story of the little man "who laughs, who has golden hair, and who refuses to answer questions."

Still, Dean continued to work, and directors

continued to seek his services. "If you knew your job," claims John Peyser, "Jimmy respected you and gave no trouble. It was a pleasure to direct him."

Pointing Dean out to a friend, director Homer Fickett said, "To look at him you wouldn't think he's playing with a full deck, but he's really quite sharp."

Such was Dean's inventiveness that he would seldom do a scene twice in the same way. He was forever experimenting, searching for ways to get deeper inside a role or make a scene come alive.

In one television show in which Dean played a young man hospitalized after a suicide attempt, he suggested he play with a toy while lying in the hospital bed. "It was a lovely touch," writer George Roy Hill remembers, "and just right for a scene that might have otherwise been somewhat on the maudlin side." Dean liked the effect so well that he later employed it again: the movie *Rebel Without a Cause* opens with Dean lying intoxicated on the sidewalk, playing with a toy monkey—the innocent youth in a cold, hard world.

But all that was still in the future; television was Dean's present metier and his career moved along without so much as the slightest setback.

The early 1950's was an exciting time in television; some would later regard it as the medium's "Golden Age." Original dramas filled the airwaves, shows like Studio One, Kraft, and Armstrong Circle Theater enjoyed great popularity.

Dean appeared on all of them, working with performers like Dorothy Gish and Ed Begley, doing scripts by promising new writers like Hill and Rod Serling.

And Dean's reputation continued to grow.

When producer Franklin Heller cast Dean in a drama with Walter Hampden, the distinguished Shakespearean actor and former president of the Players Club, it was Dean who received all the notices.

"A comparative newcomer, James Dean, stole the spotlight," *Variety* wrote, "delivering a magnetic performance that brought a routine meller alive. He's got quite a future ahead of him."

Hampden told the producer: "That young man put me on my toes and I'll wager he'll have the same effect on any other actor he works with, and though I won't live to see it, someday he'll be listed on the rostrum of truly great thespians."

At the time he said this, Hampden was in his 70's and had little more than a year to live; Dean had slightly less than two.

Chapter 8

In 1954 Dean returned to Broadway.

Terese Hayden, a talent scout who had seen Dean in *See the Jaguar* and had been closely following his work on television, recommended him to Herman Shumlin, the director. Shumlin was then casting *The Immoralist*, a dramatization of André Gide's early autobiographical novel about homosexuality.

At their first meeting Dean arrived at the director's 48th Street office on his motorcycle, wearing hip-length boots, a fringe jacket, and a huge hat. Shumlin found him "a startling sight," but he was impressed enough by Dean's audition to ask him to read again for the show's authors, Ruth and Augustus Goetz, and the producer, Billy Rose.

Dean did, and was cast as the blackmailing Arab, Bachir, in the play. The cast was small, numbering only eight actors. Louis Jourdan played a young French archaeologist tormented by guilt over his homosexuality. Geraldine Page was his wife, who naively attributes the barrenness of their relationship to a severe fever her husband contracts on their honeymoon in Africa.

Rehearsals got under way on December 18 at the old Ziegfeld building on Seventh Avenue where Rose had his offices. Almost at once Dean fell under Shumlin's spell, adopting him as a father figure. Shumlin, in turn, found the young actor a "remarkable and unusual personality whose endless variety in experimenting with his role fascinated me—up to a point. Then I decided I wanted him to stop and settle on one interpretation, which he did to my satisfaction."

But all was not entirely well. There were murmurs from other actors that Shumlin was still allowing Dean far too much freedom on stage. Paul Huber, a verteran actor who had appeared in John Barrymore's Broadway production of *Hamlet*, claims, "Dean played every scene for himself. He tried to make improvisation of the whole damn play."

Adelaide Klein, who had several scenes opposite Dean, remembers simply, "Jimmy was a tough kid to work with."

Relations did not improve any when Dean began storing his motorcycle in the cramped backstage area.

Adding to the director's problems, the Goetzes were unhappy with his treatment of their script, and they urged Rose to intervene.

Initially, the dynamic little impresario had stayed aloof from the production, explaining, "I really don't know from fairies." But as rehearsals continued to go downhill, he stepped in and fired Shumlin. "I like the cast, Herman," Rose is supposed to have said, "but I'm afraid I miscast the director."

A courtly and soft-spoken man, Shumlin bowed out graciously and was replaced by Daniel Mann, who had previously directed *The Rose Tattoo* on Broadway. Mann joined the company shortly before it left for its January tryout in Philadelphia.

The situation he inherited was precarious, and in Philadelphia Mann and the others worked around the clock to prepare for the opening.

The script was revised and a new ending written. At a cost of some $19,000, new sets were also ordered after Mrs. Goetz claimed the original scenery had left her "heartbroken."

In the rewriting Dean's part was cut, and with his mentor Shumlin gone, he now seemed to lose all interest in the production—and all sense of restraint. He clashed with the producer; he was late on cues. There were moments on stage when he went dead on the part completely. When Mrs. Goetz reprimanded him after one rehearsal, Dean told her, "I think I did all right."

As Dean had a run-of-the-play contract, Rose was reluctant to fire him, since he would have to pay him his salary of $300 a week until the play closed.

Then, after one encounter with Mann in which the director rebuked him sharply, Dean walked out of the rehearsal hall and his place was taken by his understudy. It was assumed that Dean would be automatically fired, as Equity rules permitted, but when he returned to the theater an hour later, David J. Stewart, the Equity representative, miraculously smoothed things over and Dean rejoined the cast.

"Dean was difficult to reach and totally uncooperative," Mann remembers. "In *The Immoralist* he was a destructive force. And yet at the same time he had flashes of real brilliance."

Others felt this brilliance too. "He moved like a snake," Abe Feder said. "You could literally feel the sensuality pouring over the stage."

Even so, the quality of Dean's work continued to

"He was difficult and mistrustful.
He quarreled with those around him."

A shot from the family album. Jimmy at two.

"As a child he had a large anxiety to do many things. He was always getting ahead of himself."

At Fairmount High School Dean made the baseball team his sophomore year. He played around the infield.

"It's me," Dean stammered,
"I call it 'Self.'"

On the Varsity Basketball team at Santa Monica City College.
"He was a tolerable good guard, and a leader who went for
the ball."

Dean plays Prince Malcolm in a UCLA production of *Macbeth*, Fall 1950. "Man, if I can keep this up," Dean wrote his aunt and uncle, "... one of these days I might be able to contribute something to the world (theatrically)." From left to right: Paul McKim as MacDuff, James Wasson as Banquo, Dean as Prince Malcolm.

Dean's first TV appearance. He played John the Beloved on an hour long Easter program, "Hill Number One." Spring 1951. (Seated to Dean's right is Gene Lockhart.)

Dean was a frequent visitor at the Davis home in Bel Air, from left to right: Beverly Wills, Bill Bast, Dean, Debbie Reynolds, Joan Davis.

Dean with Bill Bast's mother. "The boys welcomed her presence.... For a solid week their refrigerator was stocked with food, and the cupboard shelves groaned under the weight of newly bought groceries."

Rogers Brackett today; behind him is a portrait of himself as a young man.

Christine White: Dean wanted her for *Rebel*.

Dizzy Sheridan at the time she knew Dean. "She had a pixie sense of humor that came across in everything she said and did." And Dizzy Sheridan today.

Jimmy on West 68th Street near his apartment. "Every day he threw himself hungrily upon the world like a starving animal that suddenly finds a scrap of food. The intensity of his desires, and his fears, could make the search at time arrogant, egocentric; but behind it was such a desperate vulnerability that one was moved, even frightened."—Nicholas Ray.

On Broadway, Dean played Bachir, the blackmailing Arab in Gide's *The Immoralist*. Jimmy used shoepolish to darken his hair. Shown with Geraldine Page.

Jimmy relaxes on the set of *East of Eden*. From left to right: actor Nick Dennis, Director Elia Kazan, Dean. "There was no point in casting the part any better or nicer" Kazan later said, "He was Cal Trask."

With Julie Harris in *East of Eden*. "With affection and understanding and patience he got awfully good."

Pier visits Dean on the set at Warner s. "When he loved, he loved completely."

"At 21 Anna Maria Pierangeli was very special. She had green eyes, soft delicate features and light brown hair...." Dean told a friend: "Unlike most Hollywood girls she's real and genuine."

At Warner's commissary. There was never a dull moment. "He'd do anything to attract attention," a studio executive later said.

A rare daytime gathering at Googie's. (Now Stake & Stein) On Dean's left is Jack Simmons who appeared with him in *Rebel.*

Dean plays with cousin Markie on a visit to Fairmount after making *East of Eden.*

"Within a day he enrolled in a dance class taught by Eartha Kitt and arranged to take chess lessons."

Dean revisits Fairmount with Dennis Stock after making *East of Eden.* "It was a strange time for Jimmy," Stock later said, "I think he realized he had outgrown his past and Indiana would really never be home for him again."

With Natalie Wood in *Rebel Without a Cause*. "The legend maintained Dean was playing himself: the sensitive delinquent . . ."

A break in the action on the set of *Rebel Without a Cause*. Natalie Wood, Dean and director, Nick Ray.

"Racing is the only time I feel whole."

Dean in Times Square, winter of 1955, just before *Eden* is released. He was on the verge of fame.

Dean had his 16mm Rolex camera on location with him in Marfa.

Dean on the set of *Giant;* he also had a noose hanging in his home, chalking it up to his "macabre sense of humor."

Dean and Ursula Andress at Ciros. A quiet interlude in an otherwise stormy romance.

Dean as *Jett Rink* in *Giant*. Years later studio boss Jack Warner told designer Cecil Beaton: "That kid Dean was a natural actor. He gave us a lot of trouble, but it was worth it! He was surrounded with stars in *Giant* but we believe he was twenty-five percent responsible for the success of that picture. But boy, was he difficult!"

Dean's home at 14611 Sutton Street in Sherman Oaks. "It was built to resemble a hunting lodge...."

1 teaspoon White Karo
1 big can evaporated milk
equal part boiled water or distilled water
1 egg yoke
mix and chill
Don't feed him meat or formule cold.
1 drop vitamen solution per day
take Marcus to Dr. Cooper on Melrose for shots next week

Dean's cat Marcus, and the envelope on which Dean wrote cat's feeding formula night before his death.

Jeanette Miller and Dean.

September 20, 1955—the aftermath.

vary. Opening night in Philadelphia he was at his best, but the next night his performance was so listless that Rose stormed backstage afterwards and told him, "Don't you ever do that to me again."

The critics, however, had only been there opening night, and notices were good. The reviewer for the *Evening Bulletin* praised the production for its "restraint" and "sensitivity" and called the cast "extraordinary." Jourdan, Page, and Dean all received glowing reviews. "There is an excellent performance by James Dean as an insinuating Arab houseboy," the *Bulletin's* critic wrote, and added, "He was the caged lad in *See the Jaguar* last year, you may recall."

After three weeks in Philadelphia, the play returned to New York for a week of paid previews at the Royale Theater before officially opening.

At one preview an old friend of the Goetzes named Paul Osborn saw the play and was particularly impressed by Dean.

Osborn, a playwright (*On Borrowed Time*) and screenwriter (*Portrait of Jennie*), was at work on a movie treatment of John Steinbeck's *East of Eden*. The next day he phoned the man who was to direct the picture and told him about this young actor he had seen.

The man Osborn called was Elia Kazan.

One of the best-known directors in America, Kazan was then under exclusive contract to Warner Brothers to make a picture a year, and the studio had given him virtual carte blanche to initiate and develop his own projects.

Kazan had started out as an actor with the Group Theater in the 1930's and had appeared in several Odets plays, but later turned to directing. In 1947 he had created a sensation on Broadway with his staging of Tennessee Williams' *A Streetcar Named Desire* and had helped make an overnight star of Marlon Brando.

Since then Kazan had been alternating between Broadway and Hollywood, where he had made such films as *Man on a Tightrope*, *Viva Zapata*, and *On the Waterfront*, the last of which would soon bring him his second Academy Award as Best Director.

Dean's name was not new to Kazan; the director had seen and been impressed with Dean's audition at the Actors Studio. He had also seen Dean on television, and at one point had even considered him for the Broadway lead in *Tea and Sympathy*, playing a prep school student whose classmates falsely accuse him of homosexuality. But the role went instead to John Kerr, a Harvard graduate whose clean-cut looks better suited him to play the upper-class youngster.

Osborn's tip once again aroused Kazan's sharp casting instincts, and he now thought Dean might be just right for the part of Cal Trask, the difficult and troublesome son in the Steinbeck story.

After seeing Dean on stage, Kazan went around to talk to him. "I just got to know the guy," Kazan later said. "I hung around with him . . . and rode around on his motorcycle. I'd already made up my mind he was going to play it. I realized it wasn't a matter of could he or couldn't he; he was it."

To writer Joe Hyams, Kazan elaborated even further: "I chose Jimmy because he *was* Cal Trask. There was no point in attempting to cast it nicer or better . . . He had a grudge against all fathers. He was vengeful; he had a sense of aloneness and of being persecuted. And he was suspicious. In addition he was tremendously talented."

92

As expected, *The Immoralist* opened on Broadway to solid critical acclaim. The reviews in both the *Times* and *Herald Tribune* were favorable. "It would be hard to find serious fault with the production," wrote the *Herald Tribune*'s Walter Kerr. Only the critic for the New York *Journal-American*, a Hearst publication, struck a completely sour note, calling the play's theme "fare for a small and specialized audience."

Dean attracted by far the most attention he had to date. Reviewers for five major daily papers praised his performance. The *Times*' Brooks Atkinson claimed Dean brought "insidious charm" to the role, and even Richard Watts of *The New York Post*, whose feelings about the play were mixed, was complimentary toward Dean.

On opening night, however, as a way of getting even with Rose, Dean gave notice he was leaving the play. He took delight in posting the announcement backstage on a bulletin board. During the preceding weeks the producer had often shouted at Dean during their arguments, "This is Rose speaking." But now Dean had the last word; across the top of the paper he scrawled: "This is Dean speaking."

Dean remained with the play the required two weeks, and left the cast on February 20. Although he was out of work, he must surely have been the happiest unemployed actor in New York. Kazan and agent Jane Deacy were busy ironing out his Hollywood contract, and in the meantime he was free to do as he liked.

His aunt and uncle had come to New York to see *The Immoralist*, and Jimmy now squired them around town, proudly introducing them to his friends as "my folks from Indiana."

Never able to remain idle very long, Dean was soon involved in putting on an informal production of Sophocles' *Women of Trachis* at the New School for Social Research. The play was a new translation by Ezra Pound and had appeared in the winter *Hudson Review*. Eli Wallach and Joseph Sullivan were also in the cast, and Howard Sackler, later author of *The Great White Hope*, directed. The production was repeated at the uptown YMHA.

Then, in March, just before Dean's movie contract was finalized, Warners began to question the wisdom of using an unknown actor in such a major role. "To them," Kazan said, "it was like taking a horse from a horse and carriage and putting him in the Belmont Stakes."

To set the studio at ease, Kazan shot a brief screen test at the Gjon Mili studio in which Dean played a scene opposite costar Julie Harris.

After Warners saw the test there were no further protests. Dark horse or not, the feeling at the studio was that Elia Kazan was clearly getting set to ride home another winner.

Chapter 9

James Dean's arrival in Hollywood in the spring of 1954 was unobtrusive.

Kazan had already made clear to the studio that he wanted no build-up for the young actor, and his presence went totally unnoticed by the Hollywood press.

Dean quickly found a place to live, sharing a small $50-a-month apartment with Dick Davalos, another young actor who was in the movie. The apartment was above a drugstore in Burbank, right across the street from Warner Brothers.

Dean's salary for the picture was $10,000, and with the money the studio advanced him he bought a beautiful palomino horse, which he named Cisco and boarded at a stable in nearby Griffith Park.

As Jane Deacy did not have a West Coast office, she had arranged for the Famous Artists Agency to look after her client. The office assigned this task to Dick Clayton, one of its younger agents; the choice proved to be a wise one. Handsome and easygoing, Clayton was a former actor who had appeared in *High Sierra* and *The Wagons Roll at Night*. He knew his way around the film colony, and he knew how to handle actors. Several days after their first meeting,

Clayton arranged for Dean to buy a small sports car, an MG, and shortly thereafter Dean could be seen whizzing around town, usually accompanied by an attractive ingenue whose phone number the agent had thoughtfully provided.

Shooting for *East of Eden* began on schedule in the middle of May. Kazan and his scenarist had decided beforehand to film only the last quarter of the book, dealing with the relationship of the two Trask brothers, Cal and Aron (Cain and Abel), and their father, Adam.

Raymond Massey played the senior Trask, a pious and self-righteous man whose wife (Jo Van Fleet) had deserted him and the boys years before. Julie Harris played Abra, a young girl in love with both the Trask sons.

The rest of the fine company Kazan had assembled included Albert Dekker, Harold Gordon, Barbara Baxley, Burl Ives, and Lon Chapman. Richard Davalos, another Kazan discovery who only months before had been working as a movie usher, was cast as Aron, the more gentle Trask son, and the favorite of his father.

Warners was determined to spare no expense in mounting the production. A replica of the town of Salinas, the setting for the story, was carefully constructed on the studio lot down to the smallest detail; even the town stores were stocked with actual merchandise. A vintage 1917 train was secured from the Southern Pacific railroad for use in one scene, and for the shooting of another sequence a complete amusement park was built.

From the very start, Kazan worked closely with Dean. "Jimmy was very naked, very easily hurt,"

Kazan explained. "First I'd work with him to build up his confidence. Then I'd give him a small shove in the right direction."

The two would often go into long huddles discussing a scene, and to loosen Dean up Kazan would sometimes spar with him until the actor was ready to work. When a take still proved difficult, Kazan resorted to other means. As he later told writer Glen O'Brian, "One time we spent all afternoon on a scene and he couldn't do it, so I got him loaded on red wine that night. He couldn't drink a lot because he was sort of unstable and liquor would affect him, but I gave him two glasses of wine and he did the scene great."

The director used a number of other tricks as well: during a scene in which Adam Trask sternly reads the Bible to his sons, Kazan had Dean whisper obscenities under his breath to heighten Raymond Massey's anger. It worked very nicely.

"Working with Jimmy Dean and Raymond Massey was wonderful," Julie Harris later said. "Jimmy was very gifted . . . There was nothing he couldn't do. He was terribly interesting. He enjoyed being naughty—like Tom Sawyer. He knew his pranks upset Raymond, but they had a great feeling for each other."

"Jimmy wasn't easy because it was all new to him," Kazan explained. "He was like an animal might be. Fretful or uncertain. But with affection and understanding and patience he got awfully good. God, he gave everything he had. There wasn't anything he held back. Only at the very, very end, the last few days when you felt that a star was going to be born, and everybody smelled it, all the publicity people began to hang around him. Then he began to spoil, I thought, a little bit. By the next film I thought something in his character was spoiling."

Early in June the cast went on location for several weeks near the town of Spreckels, in the Salinas Valley. Here Kazan filmed the sequences involving Adam Trask's ill-fated lettuce refrigeration project, and also Cal's bean crop venture. Other location scenes were taken at the picturesque town of Mendocino on the coast north of San Francisco.

Dean had recently bought a Triumph T-110 motorcycle and planned to ride to Spreckels on it, but Kazan quickly vetoed the idea. "Nothing doing, Jimmy," the director told him. "I can't take a chance that you'll spill."

When the cast returned from location, Dean decided to move out of his apartment and live in his studio dressing room, a luxurious two-room suite once used by such stars as Bette Davis and Errol Flynn. Kazan, who lived in the adjoining dressing room, encouraged the move. "I kept my eye on him night and day," he said, "so we'd be sure to get through the goddamn picture."

One afternoon during a break in filming Dean wandered over to an adjacent set to visit two friends, Paul Newman and Joseph Wiseman, who were making a picture called The Silver Chalice. They introduced him to another member of the cast, a lovely Italian-born actress named Pier Angeli.

At 21, Anna Maria Pierangeli was very special. She had green eyes, delicate, almost doelike features, and light brown hair. The daughter of an engineer, Pier had been an art student in Rome before being discovered by Vittorio DeSica and becoming an actress. She had first come to Hollywood to play an Italian war bride in the movie *Teresa*, and was now living in Brentwood with her mother and two sisters, one of whom, Marisa Pavan, Pier's twin, was also an actress.

Soon Pier and Dean were visiting each other's sets daily and sharing quiet lunches in a corner of the studio commissary. Their whispering and handholding became the talk of the studio, and items about the budding romance began to appear in various columns. "James Dean has the lead in *East of Eden* and you'll be hearing of him soon," one columnist wrote. "Pier Angeli, who isn't in the movie, has discovered him already."

The items quickly came to the attention of Pier's mother, a strict, old-fashioned woman who did not consider Dean, a non-Catholic, a suitable boyfriend for her daughter. But, despite Mrs. Pierangeli's objections, the couple continued to see each other. They went for quiet early-morning horseback rides along a Hollywood trail, and Dean brought Pier to a party at Kazan's. Dean took his drums along and he and Pier played them together.

Then one evening Dean brought Pier home long after her curfew. When Mrs. Pierangeli reprimanded him, Dean told her she was "too strict" with Pier. After that Mrs. Pierangeli forbade her daughter to see Dean again, but when Pier threatened to leave home, her mother relented and the romance continued.

On Pier's twenty-second birthday she and Dean spent the day at Griffith Park washing and currying Dean's horse, Cisco.

"Pier is a rare girl," Dean told a friend. "I respect her. Unlike most Hollywood girls, she's real and genuine."

To his old friend Bill Bast, he explained: "I can talk to her. She understands."

"Jimmy is different," Pier was quoted as saying. "He loves music. He loves it from the heart the way I do. We have so much to talk about. It's wonderful to have such understanding."

Pier's influence had a strong effect on Dean. He became neater in his habits and even started to drive more carefully, as Pier disapproved of his speeding. To show his affection he showered her with presents and proudly took her home to meet his father and stepmother. "The young lion," a writer quipped, "was being tamed by love."

This sudden change in Dean both surprised and amused his friends. Actress Connie Ford recalled her amazement at seeing Dean at a dinner party wearing a navy blue suit and a smart Italian knit tie. It was the first time the actress had ever seen him with his hair combed. Pier sat next to him, looking radiant in a white chiffon dress.

On another occasion Dean even donned a tuxedo and escorted Pier to the premiere of *A Star Is Born*, a gala event held at the Pantages Theater and attended by such personalities as Marlene Dietrich and Clark Gable.

As the couple grew closer, inevitably rumors of marriage began to circulate. "Do you think eventually you kids will get married?" a reporter boldly asked Dean. "You mean me and Miss Pizza?" he replied evasively. "Who knows?"

Although he and Pier had often talked of marriage,

Dean feared being tied down and felt he was not yet ready. "I wouldn't marry her unless I could take care of her properly," he admitted. "And I don't think I'm emotionally stable enough to do so right now."

But for Pier the issue seemed simpler. "She thought if he really loved her, he would marry her," a friend said. The subject became a sore point between them, and for the first time there were quarrels and recriminations.

Late in August Dean completed his work in *Eden* and went to New York to do a TV show, the Philco Playhouse. Both Pier and the question of marriage were very much on his mind. Gusti Huber, who was in the cast, remembers Dean spoke of Pier constantly, and once during a break in rehearsal ran to Best & Co. to buy her a present.

Dean talked over his dilemma about marriage with Jane Deacy, his agent, and she advised him to wait until he was better established. From Miss Deacy's standpoint this no doubt was sound advice. She knew Dean's impulsive nature and had often cautioned him before; just a few months earlier he had even come to her wanting to change his name to Marcus Dean, but she had calmly talked him out of it.

Jimmy was away from Los Angeles only two weeks, but when he returned he sensed something had changed in his relationship with Pier.

They still saw each other, but now Pier appeared in public with other men too. Once again columnists were treated to a field day, this time chronicling the romance's demise.

Then in October Pier suddenly announced her engagement to singer Vic Damone, whom she had first met while making a picture in Germany three years before and whom she had recently been dating.

Dean was absolutely stunned. "Oh, no, please say you're kidding me," he moaned when Pier told him of her plans.

"He was deeply hurt and terribly disappointed," Bill Bast wrote. "In his persistent efforts to partake of all emotions to the fullest, when he loved, he allowed himself to love completely, and when he lost the object of his love, he allowed himself to suffer completely."

Pier was married at St. Timothy's Roman Catholic Church in Westwood on November 24. Later it was widely rumored that on Pier's wedding day Dean sat on his motorcycle outside the church, forlornly observing the proceedings. Perhaps that was just a touch of romantic hyperbole; in any event Dean was not among the six hundred guests who witnessed the ceremony inside the church, the same church where, seventeen years later, Pier's own funeral services would be held after her death, a possible suicide.

Chapter 10

With the loss of Pier, Dean found himself in very much of a limbo. *Eden* was in the final editing stage, but Warners had not yet decided on another vehicle for him. MGM wanted to borrow Dean for *The Cobweb*, a movie about a deranged artist which Vincente Minnelli was to direct, but Warners balked at the idea of their future matinee idol playing an inmate in a mental insitution.

To keep Dean busy the studio lined up several interviews, and the press got its first real look at him.

"I'm a serious-minded and intense little devil," he told Philip K. Scheuer of the Los Angeles *Times*, "terrible gauche and so tense I don't see how people stay in the same room with me. I know I wouldn't tolerate myself."

East of Eden, he informed the reporter, was "a study in dualities—that it is necessary to arrive at goodness through a sense of the Satanic rather than the puritanic ... I considered it a great challenge to reveal honestly the things in (my) part that were of myself as well as the character."

Dean went on to say: "I hate anything that limits progress or growth. I hate institutions that do this; a way of acting ... a way of thinking. I hope this doesn't make me sound like a communist. Communism is the most limiting factor of all today."

This was one of only two political statements Dean ever made; in the other he said simply that he "dug Ghandi the most."

The studio had no control over Dean's TV work, and he was signed to appear with Eddie Albert and Natalie Wood on the General Electric Theater. The show, "I'm a Fool," was an adaptation of the Sherwood Anderson story about the folly of a young man in love.

Rehearsals were held in an old theater in downtown Los Angeles, and Dean came late to work the first day. Dressed in a torn sports shirt and pants held up by a safety pin, he made his entrance by climbing through a large window. "I thought he was totally weird—until I began working with him," Natalie later said.

Former governor Ronald Reagan, then the program's host, remembers, "I was struck by how very much James Dean off camera resembled the James Dean you saw on camera. He worked very hard at his craft, rehearsed with very much the same intensity that he gave the part on camera . . . Most of us, after a while in pictures, hold back somewhat in rehearsal and save our punch for the take . . . Jimmy did not do this. He seemed to go almost all out any time that he read his lines."

Dean also began to regularly attend an acting class given in Hollywood by Jeff Corey. He participated in class exercises, Corey recalls, trying to achieve more form and control in his own work, and generously gave advice to any young actor who sought it.

Dean's social life, too, was far from empty; since

dismissed him in her column as "another dirty-shirttailed actor from New York." At Clifton Webb's suggestion, however, Hedda saw a preview of *Eden* and was totally captivated.

When Dean obediently showed up at her home for an interview, her infatuation deepened. "I want to do *Hamlet* soon," Dean told her. "Only a young man can play him as he was. Something is lost when older men play him. They anticipate his answers . . . This isn't the stumbling, searching boy that he really was."

Hedda urged that some Broadway producer give him the opportunity, and thereafter she became Dean's constant champion. "I loved that boy and I always will," she later said. Dean referred to her as "my friend at court."

As the new year approached, Warners still had not decided what Dean's next picture should be. One project under consideration was a film biography of Charles Lindbergh; another was a topical movie on troublesome adolescents to be directed by Nicholas Ray. Juvenile delinquency, then on the verge of becoming a national problem, was very much on the public's mind, and the studio recognized the appeal of a movie on the subject. But Ray had only a rough outline of the film he wanted to do and a title, borrowed from a book Warners owned the rights to: Robert Lindner's clinical study of a teenage criminal, *Rebel Without a Cause*.

Until Warners assigned him to another picture, Dean decided to return to New York to do a TV show and then visit his aunt and uncle in Fairmount. He had been approached by a young photographer named Dennis Stock, who wanted to do a story on him for *Life*, and he invited Stock to come along on the trip. Expecting to be away some time, Dean boarded his horse Cisco at a ranch in Santa Barbara owned by Lew Bracker's family.

Dean and Stock flew to New York, where Dean was scheduled to appear on the U.S. Steel Hour on January 4. The show, "Run Like a Thief," was a routine drama, but the cast was a fine one and included Mary Astor, Paul Lukas, and Diana Lynn. Nehemiah Persoff, who was also in the show, remembers Dean was nervous and remote during rehearsals. "Paul Lukas could not stand the way Dean took so much time to do his bit," recalls Persoff. "At one point, Lukas had to face Diana Lynn and say, 'Excuse me, but my son (Dean) is a little peculiar.' At dress rehearsal Dean took a great deal of time and when Lukas' turn came he said nothing. The director asked what was wrong. Lukas answered: 'I can't say my boy is peculiar; he is not peculiar. That kid is crazy.'"

Shortly after doing the show, Dean and Stock took the train to Indiana.

The trip went well; in Fairmount the prodigal was welcomed home. The local newspaper sent a reporter to interview him, and everywhere Dean went old friends and wellwishers stopped to say hello.

Dean was invited to speak at his old high school, and he gladly accepted the invitation. For an hour and a half he addressed the students as he paced back and forth, reciting Shakespeare, philosophizing, even demonstrating his bullfighting technique, enjoying himself completely. "He was just a kid showing off for the hometown folks," a teacher later said, adding with perhaps more insight than malice, "In a way, that's about all he ever was."

The one-time outcast was now king, and he savored every moment of his triumph.

As ever, the Winslows were glad to have Jimmy home once again. Aunt Ortense cooked his favorite meatloaf dinner, and each night on the table were extra helpings of mashed potatoes and stacks of fresh cornbread. Among the people he loved and trusted, Dean was open and relaxed. He had recently bought a small tape recorder, and now he secretly recorded family conversations and delighted everyone by playing them back.

For over a week Stock followed Dean around Fairmount, photographing him against the backdrop of his former boyhood haunts, trying to depict the influences and environment which had helped shape the young actor.

Dean had brought his drums along—"to see the farm animals' reactions to a primitive instrument"— and Stock photographed him sitting in a field, surrounded by a herd of cattle as he played the drums.

"It was a strange time for Jimmy," Stock later said. "I think that as much as he loved the farm and the earth around it, he realized he had outgrown his past and Indiana would never really be home for him again."

Stock's many photographs bear out this impression; in them Dean appears almost a stranger, sitting in an empty classroom in his old high school, walking alone across a frozen field, the threat of snow looming in the distance. Even in one picture taken in the family attic, where he often spent afternoons by himself as a boy, Dean has a blank look on his face, as though the surroundings had become unfamiliar.

On their last afternoon in Fairmount, Dean and Stock paid a visit to Wilber Hunt's general store, a small establishment that doubled as the town's funeral parlor. On a whim Dean climbed in one of Hunt's coffins and cajoled Stock into taking a picture. "It was the kind of joke Jimmy loved to play," a friend said. "The town thought he was nuts, but to him it was just a prank." To Dean's mild annoyance, *Life* refused to run the shot (Stock's photographic essay "Moody New Star" was published March 7, 1955), but after Dean's death the picture was printed in magazines around the world, a macabre foreshadowing of what had come to pass.

From Fairmount, Dean and Stock returned to New York. Almost from the moment he arrived in New York, Jimmy's spirits seemed to lift. Within a day he was enrolled in a class in modern dance taught by Eartha Kitt, and had arranged to take chess lessons.

Already, too, Dean was looking to the future, telling friends that he hoped to someday make a bullfight movie and to do a film biography of Woody Guthrie, the dustbowl singer, whose songs he had recently discovered.

Eventually, if Hollywood gave him the chance, Dean hoped to one day direct. He bought a Bolex .16mm camera at Dumont's on 34th Street, and began to make his own home movies, using friends like Marty Landau and Bill Gunn as actors.

"Nothing Jimmy ever did was just a sideline," said Roy Schatt, in whose small courtyard Dean made a number of movies. "He put everything he was into everything he did. In his filmmaking, he was constantly searching for the unusual, even the odd camera angle. Sometimes the results were bizarre. But they were always Jimmy."

Dean had kept his apartment while in Hollywood, and, as in the past, the small walk-up became a gathering place for his friends. There were long, late-night sessions at which Dean played his drums; conversations ranged from new movies to (as dawn broke) literature and philosophy. They read aloud stories and plays, once going right through Tennessee Williams' *27 Wagons Full of Cotton* while people took turns sleeping.

"New York is vital," Dean told Howard Thompson, a reporter for *The New York Times*. "I fit to cadence and pace better here. They're a little harder to find, maybe, but out there in Hollywood, behind all that brick and mortar, there are human beings just as sensitive to fertility. The problem for this cat is not to get lost."

But despite this sudden rush of activity Dean seemed unable to find real satisfaction in anything he did; the project of the moment might absorb him completely, but he soon grew bored and restless and moved on to something else. His old troubles and anxieties remained, and, if anything, success intensified rather than diminished them.

He was difficult and mistrustful; he quarreled with those around him. "They bum meals from me," he complained. One day in a restaurant he grew sullen. "Where are my friends?" he asked. Four of his closest friends were sitting at the table with him, but before anyone could answer he got up and walked out.

A little thing like a hitch on a telephone he was using could send him into a deep depression, but the mood might lift as completely and mysteriously as it arrived. Once a friend, Tony Ray, remembered it was cured by going to see Jacques Tati in *The Big Day*. Unshaven, hair uncombed, wrapped in his old trench-coat, Dean was morose as he entered the theater.

Within ten minutes he was laughing so wildly that others complained. Dean ignored them; the spell of laughter grew more and more irresistible. But before the film was over he had to leave, making his departure a series of hurdles over the silver ashtrays in the aisle.

For a time Dean went to an analyst, but when the sessions seemed unable to provide the relief he sought, he stopped going. Frank Corsaro tried to convince him to return, but without success. "He was never in one spot long enough," Corsaro claimed, "and he just seemed to be getting crazier by the minute."

Through a friend Dean heard that Dizzy Sheridan was in town, and when he got in touch with her, she invited him to a party. Their reunion was a happy one; Jimmy appeared overjoyed to see her, and didn't even seem to mind when Dizzy kidded him about the way he was dressed, claiming he looked "so Hollywood" in his black turtle-neck sweater.

Later Dizzy recalled: "Wherever I went at that party—if I would go into the kitchen to get food—he would follow me out there and stand and talk. Never anything about Hollywood or what he was doing but what *I* was doing, or how the old gang was. It seemed that he had just been away from home and all of a sudden he returned again and he seemed jovial on top—but very unhappy underneath, somehow."

He and Dizzy left the party together and shared a cab to Grand Central Station, where Dizzy took the train to Larchmont.

"Just before I left," she said, "he squeezed my hand in the cab and asked me if I were happy. I told him that I would be as soon as I could get back to the islands and he said, 'I know what you mean,' as if more or less he wished he had found a place to go where he could be happy."

Dizzy never saw him again; soon she left for Puerto Rico to take a job with another dance troupe and was living there when Dean died. The night she learned of his death she had just come out of a movie theater and heard a newsboy shout in the streets that James Dean had been killed in a car accident. The movie that was playing was one that had opened in San Juan a few days earlier, *East of Eden.*

In New York Dean met another old friend whom he had not seen for some time, but their reunion was less pleasant. Rogers Brackett, who had lost his job at Foote, Cone & Belding as a result of a cutback at the agency, saw Dean and over a drink asked him to loan him some money until things got better. Dean refused, saying, "Sorry, Pops." He also told Brackett that he felt he had "outgrown" him and Alec Wilder and no longer wished to be friends. To this Brackett replied, "You might outgrow me, but I don't think you can ever outgrow Alec Wilder." When told of Dean's feelings, Wilder proved equally philosophic. "That's what they all say," he shrugged.

"Probably when Jimmy was cruel or faithless," a friend explained, "he thought he was paying off an old score. The affection he rejected was the affection that had once been his and had found no answer."

By late February the city was beginning to pale for Dean; the winter had been an unusually harsh one, and he now began to talk of returning to the warmth of California.

The studio, however, was anxious for him to remain

in New York to attend the world premiere of *East of Eden* at the Astor Theater on Broadway. The evening was to be a benefit for the Actors Studio. Tickets were priced at $50 a head, and Margaret Truman and Marilyn Monroe were among the many celebrities who had agreed to serve as ushers.

But Dean refused to attend. The studio tried to get him to change his mind, but to no avail. "I can't make this scene," he told his agent, "I can't handle it."

East of Eden opened March 9 to much attendant fanfare; over 700 guests filled the theater and throngs of spectators lined the police barricades outside to glimpse the event. But unknown to them, the young star of the evening was nowhere around.

Several days earlier Dean had quietly boarded a plane and flown back to California.

Chapter 11

Back in Hollywood Dean found himself a celebrity almost overnight.

Eden had opened to great critical acclaim, with reviewers seemingly trying to outdo each other in praising Dean's performance. Writing at length in the New York *Herald Tribune*, William K. Zinnser called Dean's acting "remarkable," claiming: "Everything about Dean suggests the lonely misunderstood nineteen-year old . . . When he talks, he stammers and pauses, uncertain of what he is trying to say. When he listens, he is full of restless energy—he stretches, he rolls on the ground, he chins himself on the porch railing, like a small boy impatient of his elder's chatter . . . He has all the awkwardness of an adolescent who must ask a few tremendous questions and can only blurt them out crudely . . . You sense the badness in him, but you also like him."

Another reviewer, *The Daily News*' Kate Cameron, was more succinct: "When the last scene faded from the Astor Theater screen last night a new star appeared . . . James Dean."

As *Eden* opened at other first-run theaters across the country, more praise followed. Herb Lyon of the Chicago *Tribune* credited Dean with turning in "the performance of the year." There was a rave review in *Time*, and *Newsweek* profiled the young actor.

John Steinbeck, who had initially been unhappy with Kazan's decision to use only the latter part of the novel and had absented himself in Europe during the filming, now called *Eden* "probably the best motion picture I have ever seen."

By late March *Eden* had broken into *Variety's* list of the ten top-grossing films in the country, and soon it was number one. In several cities it set new box-office records.

But despite his new-found fame, Dean was determined not to become part of the Hollywood scene. In many ways he had never quite gotten over his bitterness at not taking Hollywood by storm after leaving UCLA, and now he was out to get his revenge. "They gave me a lot of guff out here last time," he had told Bast some months earlier. "They're not going to do it again. This time I'm going to make sure of it."

"Jimmy didn't go back to Hollywood with a chip on his shoulder," another friend, Vivian Coleman, once said. "It was a boulder."

In public, Dean was often rude and surly, sometimes deliberately so. "You're getting a lot of good publicity these days, all about your wonderful performance in *East of Eden*, a young actress told him admiringly. Dean replied: "Most of it is a bunch of shit."

"I don't know whether he was trying to compensate for his shyness or what," the girl claimed.

At the studio Dean's behavior became nearly scandalous. He refused to cooperate any further on publicity for *East of Eden*, and began giving out statements saying that acting was not the "be-all, end-all" of his existence; sports car racing was his new passion, he now proclaimed. He bought a $4,000 Porsche Speedster and let it be known he planned to enter it in local meets.

There was never a dull moment. Lunch time in the studio commissary could turn into a one-man show, with Dean clowning and banging on the table or sticking a cracker in his eye while eating. "He'd do anything to attract attention," a studio executive said. On one occasion, Dean tore his picture off the wall of the commissary, claiming he didn't want it there; another time he was seen eating alone at a table without a shirt.

Dean's behavior aroused much unfavorable attention in the film colony. Hollywood columnists characterized him as being everything from "uncouth" to "a bit mad." One wag suggested Dean's coworkers enroll him in a Dale Carnegie charm course, and a magazine editor told a photographer who had done a story on Dean, "I like the pictures, but I can't stand the subject."

Jimmy ignored his detractors. "I came to Hollywood to act, not to charm society," he said, and maintained, "the objective artist has always been misunderstood." He told Bob Thomas of the Associated Press: "I probably should have a press agent. But I don't care what people write about me. I'll talk to (reporters) I like; the others can print whatever they please."

Since moving out of his studio dressing room, Dean had been living in a one-room apartment above a garage on Sunset Strip, about a block and a half from Schwab's drugstore. The small apartment was in such disarray Dean christened it "a wastepaper basket with walls." Friends said they needed a compass to navigate across it, and one bewildered visitor claimed stepping inside was "like arriving at the scene of a hurricane."

In the evenings Dean could usually be found at Googie's, a low-priced restaurant on Sunset Strip frequented by young actors. Dressed in bluejeans and a leather jacket, Dean slumped in a booth in the rear, surrounded by a faithful group of friends. "He was like the Maypole, and they were all tied to him," Sidney Skolsky claimed. As a few beers made him woosy, Dean drank cup after cup of coffee and chain-smoked through the night.

Among the regulars in the group, known as "The Night Watch," was an attractive brunette actress named Mila Nurmi, the niece of Pavvalo Nurmi, the Finnish Olympic runner. Under the name Vampira she had become well-known playing Charles Addams-like characters on a local television show. One writer called her "the ghoul who gave people right in their own homes their daily creeps." Dean explained their friendship by saying, "I have a fairly adequate knowledge of Satanic forces and I was interested to find out if this girl was obsessed by such a force." Vampira put their mutual interests more simply: "We have the same neuroses," she explained.

Stories of Dean's eccentricities began to abound, adding to the growing legend. "I was having a soda at Googie's one evening," a pretty girl told writer Kathryn Tate. "Jimmy came in and sat down next to me. I didn't know him personally and he didn't know me. He said, 'Hi,' and started drumming on the counter with the palms of his hands. He didn't say

118

anything else until I finished my soda and got up. 'I'd like to see you again some time,' he then said. 'Can I call you or come visit you?' Frankly, I was intrigued, and gave him my telephone number and address.

"Twenty minutes later, my doorbell rang. I opened the door and there was Jimmy. He'd brought his bongo drums. He came in, sat down, started playing, and didn't stop for almost three hours. During all that time, we hardly exchanged a word. When he finished, he picked himself up as abruptly as he'd come and left. I never saw him again."

Fortunately, not everything Dean did got into print. One favorite pastime was to get together with a friend from Googie's and go around West Hollywood, trying doors until they found one that was unlocked. If no one was home, they would enter the house, make themselves coffee and fix a sandwich, eat, and then depart, leaving behind a neat stack of dishes in the sink.

Inevitably, Dean's off-beat behavior, as well as some of his mannerisms as an actor, invited comparison with another Kazan protege, Marlon Brando. "The best way to describe Jimmy Dean quickly," columnist Sidney Skolsky wrote, "is to say he is Marlon Brando seven years ago."

Of all the criticisms hurled against him, being labeled a Brando imitator disturbed Dean the most— perhaps because there was some truth in it. Ever since his early days in New York, Dean had admired Brando and had gotten to know him casually at the Actors Studio, and later at parties they both attended. New York friends recall the zeal with which Dean would rehearse scenes from *A Streetcar Named*

Desire, but they insist that even then Jimmy brought his own particular interpretation to the part of Stanley Kowalski. "Dean's Kowalski was more sensitive, more ironic," one such friend has said. "He respected Marlon as an actor—who didn't?—but it wasn't the hero worship the fan magazines and publicists claimed. Dean was an individualist, an original, and anyone who came into contact with him felt it." Christine White, who knew both Dean and Brando, claimed: "It was a coincidence of nature that they were from the same mold."

Brando, however, disliked Dean from the beginning, and after *East of Eden* was released, accused him of "wearing my last year's wardrobe and using my last year's talent in the movie."

Such comments stung Dean, although he tried not to show it. "When a new actor comes along he's always compared to someone else," he told Bob Thomas. "Brando was compared to Clift, Clift to someone else, Barrymore to Booth and so forth . . . I can only do the best job I can, the realist acting. They can compare me to W.C. Fields if they want to."

But when the comparisons between him and Brando continued, Dean's responses grew icier and more in character. "I was riding a motorcycle long before I heard of Mr. Brando," he pointedly informed one reporter. To another, he announced: "People were telling me I behaved like Brando before I knew who Brando was. I am neither disturbed by the comparison, nor am I flattered by it. I have my own personal rebellions and don't have to rely on Brando's . . . Within myself are expressions just as valid . . . And I'll have a few years to develop my own—what shall I say?—style."

The studio was equally eager for Dean to develop this style, and was ready to give him the opportunity. He was awarded a new contract calling for nine pictures over a six-year period, with the guarantee he would receive a minimum of $15,000 per picture. The year 1956 was to be open for him to do a Broadway play, and he was free to do any TV work he wanted.

Once the new contract was finalized, Dean was assigned to *Rebel Without a Cause*, which had long been rumored as his next vehicle.

Although preliminary work had been underway on the picture for almost six months, director Nicholas Ray had already had his share of production difficulties. Two early story treatments, including one by Ray himself, had proved unsatisfactory, and he was still without a workable screenplay. Moreover, there were rumblings from the Breen office that any frank treatment of juvenile delinquency might result in denial of a production code seal. At Warner's, one or two front-office executives were privately leery about the whole project; some on the lot doubted the film would ever be made. One enterprising technician had even made a sizeable bet to that effect.

But Ray was determined to move forward nevertheless.

A talented though mercurial man, then in his early 40's, Ray had had a checkered career before finding his niche as a Hollywood director. He had been at different times a radio script writer in his native Wisconsin, a student of Frank Lloyd Wright's, and a Broadway director, before Elia Kazan hired him and took him to Hollywood as his assistant.

Since leaving Kazan, Ray had made a number of

notable films of his own, including *They Live by Night*, *In a Lonely Place*, and *Knock on Any Door*, the last based on Willard Motley's best-selling novel about an adolescent who drifts into crime as a result of poverty.

Not wanting to repeat himself, Ray now decided to approach the subject of juvenile delinquency from a different angle, focusing upon middle-class youths whose feelings of isolation and aimlessness placed them at odds with their families and the society around them. It was a theme which was to strike an immediate responsive chord with youthful filmgoers everywhere; bobby socks and penny loafers would quickly give way to the era of blue denim and leather jackets.

To successfully work with Dean, Ray sensed he needed to create "a special kind of climate. He needed reassurance, tolerance, and understanding," the director later wrote. "I leveled with him all the time and made him feel a part of the entire project. He wanted to belong and I made him feel that he did."

Hoping to win Dean's confidence, Ray often invited him to drop by his house on Sunday afternoons to meet his friends and talk. Ray was then living in a small cottage at the Chateau Marmont, and these gatherings included friends like Joe Pasternak, the producer, and screenwriter Joan Harrison, who was Alfred Hitchcock's assistant. "It was exploratory on both sides," Ray said. "Was he going to like my friends, would he find their climate encouraging? Both of us had to know."

One Sunday, after the others had left, Dean found himself face to face across an empty room with Clifford Odets.

"I'm a son of a bitch," Dean said quietly. Odets asked why. "Well," Dean explained, "here I am in this room. With you. It's fantastic. Like meeting Ibsen or Shaw."

Odets afterward remembered this as one of the most charming remarks ever addressed to him.

Another afternoon, Dean met Irving Shulman, who was then working on the screenplay for *Rebel*. Shulman had recently replaced Leon Uris, who had dropped out of the project. Reworking the script, Shulman had already made one valuable contribution, the so-called "chickie run" scene. This was based on a newspaper story the author read. According to the story, a group of teenagers had assembled in stolen cars on a cliff overlooking the ocean. Drivers were to race each other toward the edge, and the first to jump from the car before it went over was a "chickie." On this particular night one of the teenagers failed to jump.

Knowing Shulman was a sports car buff, Ray hoped an immediate rapport would be forthcoming between him and the young actor. The result, however, was disappointing. Dean was dismayed to discover that Shulman's car, an MG, lacked special carburetors for racing and did not have real wire wheels; for his own part, Shulman felt it was "still a little too close to World War II" to appreciate Dean's German-made Porsche.

Not long after, Shulman himself dropped from the project to work on a novel; his place was taken by a younger writer named Stewart Stern, and work progressed rapidly.

In the press there was lively speculation as to who would costar opposite Dean. Hedda Hopper reported that both Debbie Reynolds and Lori Nelson were under consideration, and another young actress, a comely alumna of Southern Methodist University named Jayne Mansfield, also had tested for the role.

Dean's choice was Christine White, his old friend from the Actors Studio, but ultimately the part went to Natalie Wood, with whom Dean had also worked and liked. A one-time child actress, Natalie was then only sixteen.

Another former child actor, Sal Mineo, was cast as Plato, the lonely, neurotic youngster whom Dean befriends in the movie. Dean had wanted Jack Simmons, one of the crowd at Googie's, but after meeting Mineo at Ray's apartment, the two warmed to each other and Mineo won Dean's approval.

In choosing the rest of the cast, Ray also did his best to select actors Dean felt comfortable with.

Nick Adams, a friend from Dean's early days in Hollywood, was signed to play a young gang member, as was Dennis Hopper, an eighteen-year-old actor whom the studio had first spotted playing an epileptic on "Medic" and awarded a contract.

Jack Simmons was given a bit part, and Dennis Stock, still another member in good standing of the Dean entourage, became dialogue coach.

Among the "non-club" members Ray chose were Ann Doran and Jim Backus, who played Dean's parents. Rochelle Hudson was cast as Natalie's mother, and Bill Hopper, Hedda's son, played the father.

By the middle of March casting was completed and shooting on the movie was scheduled to start at the end of the month.

Before beginning work on the picture, however, Dean planned to enter his first sports car race, an event he had long looked forward to. The meet, to be held in Palm Springs, was sponsored by the California Sports Car Club, an association of amateur and professional drivers.

When the studio got wind of Dean's plans, there was some apprehension in the front office, but director Ray was unalarmed. "I encouraged his racing," he later said. "I felt it was good for Jimmy to do something on his own with clarity and precision."

The weekend of the race Dean drove to Palm Springs, accompanied by Lili Kardell, a lovely Swedish-born actress whom he had been dating. They planned to stay in a small house in the desert, owned by Dick Clayton, Dean's agent, who was also going to be there with his date.

The morning of the race was hot, without so much as a light breeze to stir the desert air. A field of 19 cars was entered into the competition, a rugged six-lap race over a 2.3 mile circuit set up along the concrete runways of the Palm Springs Airport.

Dressed in black racing coveralls and wearing a checkered cap, Dean was in high spirits waiting for the event to begin. "Racing," he would later say, "is the only time I feel whole."

Dean's starting position, drawn by lot, was in the fourth row back, virtually buried behind the rest of the pack. But as the flag fell Dean jammed his right foot down on the gas pedal and roared away to a perfect Texas start, "stampeding" past a number of other cars by cutting wide around the outside.

"No one expected Dean to go like he did," observed Wilson Springer, a Los Angeles sports car enthusiast. "He went out and left everyone. He was really blasting . . . going like a bomb."

At the first quarter mile Dean had maneuvered the

car into fifth place, and before the first lap ended he had taken the lead. On the long back straightway Dean was clocked at 100 miles an hour, the top limit the Porsche could go.

For the remaining five laps Dean easily held the lead, finally taking the checkered flag with almost a full quarter lap separating him and the runner-up.

"He was a lead foot, hard on engines, but he wasn't afraid of the devil," claims author William Nolan, who was there that day. "Even while charging through the pack his face was expressionless. Some drivers frowned, gritted teeth, etc. But not Jimmy. He was totally cool at speed."

In ceremonies following the race, Dean was awarded a handsome silver trophy.

"At first we had thought he was just some Hollywood character out for cheap publicity, but he earned our respect," another driver conceded. "He proved himself one helluva fine driver."

Boosted by his victory, Dean entered another event, open only to professional drivers, and held the next day.

Racing in a much tougher field of competition, Dean finished third behind two top veteran drivers, Ken Miles and Cy Yedor. For his performance, Dean won two more silver trophies: one for his overall third-place finish, and another for taking second in his particular class (cars from 1,100—1,500 cc).

In this race, however, Dean's daredevil elan drew sharp reproach from other drivers. "His skill was a dangerous one," a fellow competitor said. "The kind that comes from a desperate desire to win. He was a menace to himself and other drivers. He would take any kind of chance to be first."

And Ken Miles, an Englishman who was later killed racing at Riverside, summed up Dean's driving this way: "Jimmy wanted speed. He wanted his body to hurdle across the ground, the faster the better. Jimmy was a straightaway driver. His track was the shortest distance between here and there."

But, the race completed and trophies in hand, Dean had other things to think about than the carping of drivers he had handily battled on the track.

That night he had to be back in Hollywood. The next day, Monday, March 28, Dean had an early date at the studio; shooting on *Rebel Without a Cause* was set to begin.

Chapter 12

Of his three films, *Rebel Without a Cause*, of course, was the one Dean was most closely identified with. As *Casablanca* was the ultimate Bogart movie, so *Rebel* became the quintessential Dean film—the one in which, the legend maintained, Dean was playing himself: the sensitive delinquent, the original crazy mixed-up kid who, as Pauline Kael put it, "does everything wrong because he cares so much."

The legend was not altogether untrue; so many of Dean's mannerisms—the soft, hesitant drawl, the cigarette butt dangling from his lips, his perpetual slouch—went into the film that it was difficult to tell where his own personality left off and acting took over. "When you saw *Rebel Without a Cause*" Dennis Stock said, "that was Jimmy you were seeing up there on the screen."

Much of the movie was shot on location in and around the Los Angeles area, using such familiar sights as Santa Monica High School, the Hollywood jail, and the D.W. Griffith Observatory, where some of the film's most famous scenes were taken. The deserted mansion sequence was shot in the same house that was used for the movie *Sunset Boulevard* in which William Holden wooed Gloria Swanson.

Now torn down, the old mansion was actually located on Wilshire Boulevard and Crenshaw.

On the set Dean immersed himself in his role with his usual gusto, sometimes losing himself in the part completely. To key himself up for a scene, he would jump up and down, shadow box, and wave his arms wildly. "He throws everything into his acting," costar Natalie Wood told writer Jack Holland, "and I have bruises on my arm to prove it."

Before doing a difficult scene, Dean would refuse to speak to other actors and demanded total silence on the set, so as not to disturb his concentration. "In the morning when he'd come to work, you could say, 'Hello, Jimmy,' and he'd walk right by you," Dennis Hopper remembers. "But he wasn't really ignoring you . . . His approach was to shut the door, and don't bother with anyone . . . Just get down to work, because work was the important thing."

More than once, however, Dean held up shooting and delayed production, refusing to work until he was ready. Before doing one scene, in which he was brought into Juvenile Hall on a drunk and disorderly charge, Dean kept the cast and crew waiting an hour while he sat alone in his dressing room, drinking wine and playing his drums to get in the right mood. "What the hell does he think he's doing?" one crew member grumbled. "Even Garbo never got away with that."

When Dean was finally ready, he stormed out, strode onto the set, and did the seven-minute scene in one take.

Throughout the filming Ray continued to allow Dean as much freedom as possible in interpreting his role. "Lack of sympathy, lack of understanding from a director disoriented him completely," Ray later wrote. "To work with him meant exploring his nature, trying to understand it; without this his powers of expression were frozen."

When one particular sequence, a scene in which Dean quarrels with his father (played by Jim Backus), seemed to be causing trouble, Ray invited Dean over to his house one evening to work on it there. When Dean arrived, Ray stationed himself before a television set, switching to a blank screen, so that he could watch Dean unobtrusively as he roamed around, snatched a bottle of milk from the refrigerator, and thought himself slowly into the situation. After Dean had the scene as he and Ray wanted it, Ray got the set designer to come over to his house so that the living room set could be replaced on the lines of his own; the next day the sequence was shot exactly as Dean and the director had rehearsed it, down to the bottle of milk and the blank television screen which shimmered in the background.

In another scene, a knife fight between Dean and a young gang member, Dean insisted that real knives be used to create the proper atmosphere of tension and danger the situation called for. Over protests from studio officials, Ray backed Dean up; real switchblades were used, and though the actors wore chest protectors under their shirts, Dean received a slight cut on the neck. This filled him with a strange feeling of satisfaction, Royston Ellis wrote, a feeling of having "lived the part," rather than only acted it.

(Though awarded a production code seal, the film was later condemned in various quarters because of its violence. Writing in *The New York Times* (October 27, 1955) Bosley Crowther described the movie as "brutal . . . and excessively graphic," and claimed, "It's a picture to make the hair stand on end." In Memphis, Tennessee, the local censor board banned the film as being "inimical to the public welfare," and in England, where Dean had numerous fans, it was several years before *Rebel Without a Cause* was allowed to be shown.)

Dean also insisted upon doing his own stunts, even though the production department feared an injury to him might hold up shooting and cost the studio thousands of dollars. In the famous "chickie-run" scene Dean was to leap from a car just before it went over a cliff. The scene was shot at the Burbank studio, and though the car was stationary, Dean refused the use of a mattress to help ease his fall. Limey, the studio prop man, assured Dean that Errol Flynn had used the same mattress in some of his most dauntless screen feats, but the argument fell on deaf ears. "Take it away, Limey," Dean told him. "People will say, 'Jimmy Dean can't even do his own stunts, he needs a mattress.' "

Despite the seriousness with which he approached his role, out of camera range Dean remained unpredictable as ever. "The one thing he could be expected to do was the unexpected," a journalist later noted.

Crossing the Warners lot with Stewart Stern after work, Dean was stopped by Warner executive Steve Trilling and another man. "Here's somebody I want you to meet, Jimmy," Trilling said.

Dean stared at the ground, and acknowledged the introduction by taking some coins from his pocket and tossing them in front of Trilling. Then he walked away.

Afterwards, he said to Stern, "Stu, I'd like you to

do me a favor. If you ever find out why I acted the way I did today, please tell me."

In other moods, however, Dean would graciously talk with fans who visited the set, and gladly posed with them for photographs. Once, he delighted a group of visitors by signing autographs to their hearts' content while sitting in an empty trash can.

Dean would also entertain others on the set with his excellent imitations, doing Chaplin, Elia Kazan, or Montgomery Clift with equal ease.

One take-off he did on Mr. Magoo, the radio character made famous by Jim Backus, was so good Ray had it written into the script. "He became other people with obvious passion," Ray said. "This was a great part of his magic as an actor."

Along with his pal, Nick Adams, Dean even worked up a comedy routine, and when word got out about it, the two were approached by a Las Vegas talent scout interested in signing them for a nightclub act. Jimmy promised to give it some thought. "It's a lot of money," he told Adams, "and not much work."

Not that Dean lacked other opportunities to pick up a few quick dollars. Early in May, during a break in *Rebel*, he was paid $2,500 for appearing in "The Unlighted Road" on the Schlitz Playhouse of Stars. Dean played a young ex-GI who unwittingly becomes mixed up in a hijacking ring. The show, which turned out to be Dean's last television appearance, costarred Pat Hardy. Producer William Self remembers only that "Dean came to work on a motorcycle, and acted extremely casual about everything but gave us no trouble."

If Dean could be so relaxed, it was certainly with good reason. He was currently the most sought-after young actor in Hollywood; scripts piled up for him to read, and producers vied to offer him roles. MGM, which had failed to get Dean for *The Cobweb*, now wanted him to play Rocky Graziano in *Somebody Up There Likes Me*, the movie adaptation of the prize fighter's best-selling autobiography. And producer Lew Kerner approached Dean about portraying Studs Lonigan on the screen. Nor were these the only roles believed to be in the offing; even a brief visit the actor made one afternoon to another studio was enough to set off a fresh flurry of rumors. The fact that he was there to see the studio dentist made no difference.

Warners, though, had no intention of loaning Dean out to another studio right now. Although *Rebel Without a Cause* still had several weeks of shooting left, the studio already had firm plans of its own for Dean's next picture. This was to be *Giant* an all-star vehicle, which George Stevens planned to direct and coproduce.

Based on Edna Ferber's popular saga of a Texas family, the film was to star Elizabeth Taylor, Rock Hudson, and Dean and to feature a fine supporting cast that included Mercedes McCambridge, Jane Withers, Rod Taylor, Carroll Baker, Paul Fix, and Chill Wills. Dean was to play Jett Rink, a bitter and ambitious ranch hand who, through good fortune and a gambling instinct, becomes a multimillionaire. The part, supposedly loosely based on the career of Glen McCarthy, the flamboyant Houston oilman and builder of the Shamrock Hotel, was a real plum, and for Dean a departure from playing what one writer called "sinister adolescents."

But if the studio had any hopes that Dean's

growing stature as an actor might somehow alter his behavior, they were soon sorely disappointed. At a luncheon given to introduce the cast of *Giant* to the press, it was the same old Dean who showed up late dressed in bluejeans and his favorite red flannel shirt. When a photographer asked him to pose for a shot, Dean clipped on his sunglasses and refused to remove them, explaining he had been up late and had bags under his eyes.

Dean also continued to avoid the usual Hollywood social scene, preferring instead the company of cronies like Lew Bracker, stunt driver Bill Hickman, and Bill Stevens, a sports car driver who was then sharing Dean's apartment.

Stevens had a girlfriend who was a secretary, and he and Dean often double dated, with Dean going out with one of her friends. Stevens, who afterward became an actor, always looked with amusement on stories that linked Dean romantically with Natalie Wood. "Natalie was just a little girl then," Stevens said. "Jimmy and I used to walk her home from high school."

But Dean's favorite date remained Lili Kardell, whose lively outlook and cheerful anti-establishment attitude closely resembled his own. "With Jimmy nothing was ever planned; everything had to be spontaneous," remembers Lili. "I would get on the back of his motorcycle and he would go like hell." Knowing the way to her man's heart, Lili, who is now an interior decorator in New York, once sent Dean as a gift a new oil filter for his Porsche.

Always on the lookout for a new home away from home, Dean began to take his meals at the Villa Capri, a small Italian restaurant located on McCadden

Place, half a block from Hollywood Boulevard. The maitre d', Nicolas Romanos, was something of a character in his own right. An engaging White Russian emigre, Romanos claimed to have once been a dancer with the Diaghilev Ballet and to have hobnobbed with various legendary figures as a young man in Paris.

The first time Dean came to the restaurant and asked what was good on the menu, Romanos told him, "How should I know? I hate Italian food. Go down the street to Don the Beachcomber's if you want a good meal." After that, Romanos quickly became both Dean's friend and confidant, and the Villa Capri his new hangout.

Dean invariably entered the restaurant by coming in through the kitchen, first stopping to sample the antipasto the chef kept in the refrigerator. If the restaurant was crowded, Dean simply sat at a table reserved for someone else. Finally Romanos resolved matters by fixing up a small storeroom off the kitchen where the actor could eat. Sitting there on an empty orange crate, he enjoyed his veal parmigiana apart from the other diners.

Dean's eccentricities, however, were no longer much of a novelty. Fewer eyebrows were raised when he sauntered into his favorite places unshaven and wearing his dirtiest clothes. At the Villa Capri Dean might sit alone for an hour, carefully building a house out of breadsticks, but no one paid much attention. What had once been ways of expressing his identity now seemed only a calculated pose to get attention.

There were some, of course, who felt this was what Dean had been up to all along. "He was always conscious of his image," a director claimed, "and he worked very hard to maintain it."

"Dean could behave intelligently when it suited

him," explains Walter Ross, who was then a publicity man at the studio. "If there was something important he wanted to talk to you about, he expressed himself clearly, but after he told you what he wanted, all you would get from him was mumbles. It made you wonder." Ross, who eventually left Warners to go out on his own, later wrote a novel, *The Immortal*, in which the main character, a brash young actor, reminded many of Dean.

But now even some of Dean's closest friends were beginning to be put off by his antics. "It was the same game he had been playing for two years," declared Bill Bast. "I was embarrassed by his lack of inventiveness and it bored me."

Although Bast's affection for his friend still remained, other friendships proved not quite so durable. There was a falling-out with Vampira, and Dean's friendship with Leonard Rosenman, a young composer who had scored *East of Eden*, cooled. Rosenman, who was then engaged in scoring *Rebel*, had once been as close to Dean as anyone; at one point the two had talked about Dean directing a one-act opera, *Cipolla the Great*, that Rosenman had written, but this too died with the friendship. Even after Dean's death, some of the bitterness lingered. "Jimmy was always saying how he loathed Hollywood," Rosenman told writer Martin Mayer, "but really he loved it. You know how it is, in the land of the blind the one-eyed man is king. In Hollywood, Jimmy could believe he was an *intellectual*."

Shooting on *Rebel Without a Cause* was completed the last week in May, and Dean immediately reported to start work on *Giant*. Stevens and the other principals in the cast planned to leave on the 27th of the month for Charlottesville, Virginia, where the movie was to be on location for two weeks. Since Dean was not needed for any scenes to be shot there, Stevens arranged for him to remain behind, getting outfitted for his wardrobe, and working with dialogue coach Bob Hinkle to perfect a Texas accent. Dean was then to catch up with the others in Marfa, Texas, where principal location work was scheduled to begin early in June.

Once again, however, the subject of Dean's racing came up. Several weeks earlier, midway through *Rebel*, he had shaken front-office executives by entering his car in a Sunday meet at Bakersfield. Driving on a rain-slicked track, Dean won two trophies in an afternoon that was marred by a crash in which a 32-year-old driver, Jack Drummond, lost his life. When a reporter asked Dean how Warners felt about his racing, he replied: "They sort of shoot around it, but they've never said, 'Don't do it.' Everybody likes a winner, and so far I've been winning."

But now Stevens put his foot down. A five-million-dollar production was at stake and Stevens had no intention of jeopardizing it for Dean's love of speed: during *Giant* Dean was forbidden to race or to take his Porsche with him to Texas as he had hoped. He had told the director he wanted to use the car to hunt rabbits, but in Marfa Dean would have to find other means for getting around on the range.

Although he had given his word to Stevens, Dean conveniently managed to stretch his side of the agreement. Memorial Day Weekend (May 28—29) there was a race being run in Santa Barbara, and he decided to compete in it, though work in *Giant* was officially underway.

Accompanied by Bill Stevens, his friend and mechanic, Dean drove to Santa Barbara the day before the race and checked into the Del Mar Hotel.

The next morning Jimmy was at the track early. "I saw him at the technical inspection," said driver Dave Watson. "He was . . . off to the side by himself. He was very interested in the other cars. I could tell he didn't miss a trick."

But luck was not to be with Dean that weekend. He drew a poor starting position, finding himself 18th behind the leader at the pole.

Pushing hard from the outset, Dean maneuvered his car through the crowded field, moving ahead until another Porsche suddenly cut in front, nearly brushing his bumper. Dean swerved to avoid a crash and sideswiped two of the packed hay bales, skidded for several feet, and came to a halt. According to William Nolan, who witnessed the event, only Dean's quick reflexes and thinking averted a catastrophe.

Immediately Dean resumed his former pace, and by the fifth lap he had moved into fourth place, gaining rapidly on the leader. But Dean was pressing too hard, and his engine blew under the strain. With a single lap remaining, he coasted to a halt at the side of the track, his dicing at an end. The race was won by Dale Johnson, a driver Dean had beaten at Palm Springs.

Back in Hollywood, Dean had no time for bitter reflection. With only a week left before he was due in Marfa, Dean settled down to the serious business of tackling his role. He read up on Texas history and studied a tome on cattle raising. He put his tape recorder to good use as well, spending hours going over his dialogue.

The part of Jett Rink, Dean freely admitted, was the hardest challenge he had yet faced. Still, on the eve of his departure his enthusiasm remained high. "George Stevens is the greatest director of them all—even greater than Kazan," he asserted. "Stevens was born for the movies. You know, when it wants to, Hollywood can accomplish tremendous things. And this movie might be one of them."

This was indeed heady praise, and a rare song for Dean to sing, but down in Marfa there would be a more familiar tune.

Chapter 13

Fifty-nine miles from the Mexican border, and three and a half hours by car from El Paso, the nearest city of any size, Marfa was a typical sleepy Southwest town. The population was approximately 2,900, the mayor, Henry A. Coffield, had recently been reelected to office without opposition, and the surrounding area, Presidio County, was in the grips of a severe drought.

Some 280 strong, including technicians and actors, the company of *Giant* poured into town, bringing with them over a million dollars' worth of equipment to mount the production. To capture the flavor of life among the Texas rich, the studio imported a fleet of expensive automobiles, including a grand 1924 Rolls Royce touring car. An entire three-story Victorian mansion, which had been built at the studio in Burbank, was shipped to Marfa in sixty sections and reassembled on a ranch seventeen miles outside of town. Costing $200,000, the building was used only for exteriors and remained behind after the filming; the ranch's proprietor, Ward Evans, later converted it into a hay barn.

Ironically, as Marfa was situated in an area of West Texas that produced no oil, the company erected

140

their own wells, machines that gushed over 2,200 gallons a minute of ersatz oil. To simulate a dust storm for one scene, a gigantic wind machine was also constructed, but here Marfans were on more familiar ground and remained unimpressed. One old timer who had seen many a real duster called the Hollywood facsimile "a pretty puny attempt," complaining it hardly stirred up "more than four acres of soil."

But generally relations were good between outsiders and their hosts. Edna Ferber's novel, which some had thought a *roman à clef* about the King Ranch, had not been popular among Texans, who considered it an unflattering portrait of their state, and the film company was prepared to go to great lengths to insure local harmony. The set was thrown wide open to visitors, who came from all over the state to see the filming, in some cases timing their summer vacations so they could make the trip.

To further cement good relations, a former rodeo queen from the University of Texas was signed for a cameo, and in one barbecue scene, among the sixty-five extras, it was said that ten were authentic Texas millionaires. One, Fayette Yates, happily announced that he had finally fulfilled a lifelong ambition to be an "actor." The pride of Texans was a serious matter and would not be treated lightly by their Hollywood brethren.

In Marfa, this strategy worked especially well. Altogether almost two hundred Marfans went on the company payroll, including the town's lone bootblack, whom director Stevens personally invited to be in the movie, "along with Rock and Liz." He played a train porter.

The town's weekly newspaper, *The Big Bend*

Sentinel, which had once denounced Edna Ferber's novel as "superficial and derogatory to Texans," now was won over to the side of the angels: "The filming of *Giant* has brought invaluable publicity to Marfa," a writer neatly explained, "in addition to putting many thousands of dollars in circulation."

Although Stevens retained the good will of Marfans throughout the filming, achieving peace within his own company proved somewhat of a different matter.

The movie was on location slightly more than two weeks when the first reports of dissension between Stevens and Dean filtered back to Hollywood.

Then 51 years old, George Stevens had a solid reputation as a Hollywood director, having made such movies as *A Place in the Sun*, based on Dreiser's *An American Tragedy*, and *Shane*. A one-time cameraman who had first broken into movies shooting Laurel and Hardy comedies, Stevens' directorial method was both expensive and time-consuming—as well as enormously successful. Known as the "round the clock" system, Stevens would shoot a scene from every conceivable angle and spend up to a year editing the footage, selecting the best frames for his final print. (On *Giant* over 600,000 feet of film were shot, of which 25,000 were used.)

On the set Stevens was regarded as a taskmaster who had firm ideas of how a scene should be done and very little patience for actors' vagaries. Dean, on the other hand, worked best in an informal atmosphere, one in which he was free to improvise.

"When an actor plays a scene exactly the way a director orders, it isn't acting. It's following instructions," Dean maintained. "Anyone with the physical qualifications can do that. (An actor) must be allowed the space, the freedom, to express himself in the role. Without that space an actor is no more than an unthinking robot with a chestful of push buttons."

In *Rebel Without a Cause* Nick Ray had allowed him such freedom and achieved fine results. But Stevens had no intention of permitting his 24-year-old star any such liberties. "They'd meet head on," an actress later remembered, "and there'd be a terrible clash."

In recounting his experiences in working with Dean to a magazine reporter, Stevens had this to say: "(Dean) had the ability to take a scene and break it down; sometimes he broke it down into so many bits and pieces that I couldn't see the scene for the trees, so to speak. I must admit that sometimes I underestimated him, and sometimes he overestimated the effects he thought he was getting . . . All in all it was a hell of a headache to work with him . . . It's tough on you, he'd seem to imply, but I've just got to do it this way. From the director's point of view that isn't the most delightful sort of fellow to work with . . ."

Frustrated by his lack of rapport with Stevens, Dean quickly lost interest in the production. He avoided the rushes, which were shown each evening at a local theater the company took over, and absented himself from social gatherings attended by the rest of the cast. At one barbecue he did go to, Dean filled his plate with fried chicken and repaired to a cowshed, only emerging after most of the others had left.

Rock Hudson, who was assigned the same living quarters as Dean, later complained that he never got "a single pleasant word" from him. According to one account, Hudson hadn't forgotten that Dean was once a bit player in a movie he had starred in, and resented the attention Dean was receiving in the press. But whatever the reasons, the dislike was clearly mutual. "He was nasty, mean," Hudson told reporter Maurice Zolotow. "I don't know what was eating him. If I said hello or good morning he snarled at me."

With several exceptions, Dean's relations with others in the company were not much better. Chill Wills, who also had been bunking with Hudson and Dean, soon moved out after an argument over Jimmy's playing a guitar. A man of few words, Wills had taken the guitar and broken it. "It was a cheap ol' guitar," the veteran character actor commented afterward, by way of apology. "Blame thing couldn't have cost him more than six bucks."

Fortunately, Dean had a number of allies on the set. Dennis Hopper, his friend from *Rebel*, had a supporting role in *Giant* and was also on location in Marfa. Six years Dean's junior, Hopper had grown up on a small Kansas farm, and their similar background drew him and Dean together despite the age difference. "It wasn't a buddy-buddy hang-out thing," Hopper later explained. "But he knew I was really interested in acting and film, and it became sort of like student and teacher between me and Jimmy."

On *Rebel* Dean had offered Hopper an occasional acting tip, introducing him to fundamental Method techniques. "If you're smoking a cigarette, smoke the cigarette and don't *act* (it)," Dean had told him. "You have to do something and not show it."

But in Marfa he began watching Hopper's takes, sometimes without Hopper's knowing it, and afterward they'd go over the take together.

"He was the most creative person I ever knew," Hopper later said, "and he was twenty years ahead of his time."

Dean's self-assurance before the cameras also impressed his young protege. "Jimmy would come on the set and literally give everybody the finger and make them his enemy," Hopper told an interviewer for *Gallery* magazine. "Then he wouldn't have to hear from the grips about how James Cagney would have played that scene or listen to all the advice a young actor would have to stand . . . from the crew."

So great was Dean's influence that after his death Hopper seemed determined to carry on in his friend's footsteps. He moved to New York to enroll in the Actors Studio and remained there two years. When he returned to Hollywood to make a Western, he quickly earned a reputation as being difficult to direct. As a result, Hopper worked very little over the next decade, landing only an occasional part in low-budget productions (*Night Tide*, *The Trip*), until he teamed with Peter Fonda to direct and act in *Easy Rider*. The movie grossed millions and made Hopper a star in his own right, though in numerous interviews he always acknowledged his debt to Dean, faithfully maintaining his position as Dean's self-appointed heir to this day.

But Dean's influence had more immediate results as well. Inspired by his friend's, Hooper sometimes resisted Stevens' suggestions, wanting to play a scene his own way. This did not please the director. "You've been watching that Dean again," Stevens would tell Hopper sternly. "You guys are screwing me up."

Elizabeth Taylor, who was having her own share of differences with Stevens, likewise found a friend in

Dean. Originally, Stevens had wanted Grace Kelly for the movie, but when she proved unavailable, he turned to Liz instead. He had directed her in *A Place in the Sun* and had gotten a good performance from her as a spoiled heiress, but her role in *Giant* was far more demanding. She played a woman who ages thirty years in the course of the film, going from an eighteen-year-old belle to a grandmother of two; at the time Liz was only twenty-two, which made the latter transitions in age that much harder to portray. (Carroll Baker, who played her daughter in the movie, was twenty-four.)

Like Dean, Liz found herself at odds with the director from the very beginning. "I found out on *Giant*," she later explained, "that (Stevens) tends to like having a patsy or two on a film. Jimmy Dean was one and I was another, but I'll say this for George—he usually picks people who can answer back."

One early skirmish took place over a costume Stevens had selected for her. Liz claimed the heavy stockings and large hat the director had chosen made her look mannish. Stevens charged that all she cared about was how she looked, and her only concern was in "being glamorous." "There was a huge battle," Liz remembers. "I think I got rid of the hat. Nobody won; nobody lost; we did the scene. It was like that during the whole film."

Liz's friendship with Dean did not go unnoticed by the Hollywood press. Her marriage to English actor Michael Wilding, her second husband, was known to be on shaky grounds, and reporters in Marfa, seeing her and Dean having dinner at a local country club or strolling through the streets of town, hinted at a possible romance. Others, however, believed there was not much substance to the rumors. According to

John B. Allan, one Taylor biographer, her friendship with Dean was similar to the one she enjoyed with Montgomery Clift, with whom she had made *A Place in the Sun* and who had remained her dearest friend. "If the relationship with Clift was like two cousins who'd met after both had grown up," Allan wrote, "the relationship with Dean was more like two in-laws, neither of whom can stand the rest of either family."

Most of Dean's free time, however, was spent in the company of Bob Hinkle, the cast's dialogue coach. Before the start of the picture Hinkle had worked with the actor on his accent, and in Texas the friendship deepened. "People told me he was moody and hard to get along with, that he clamped up and wouldn't talk," Hinkle said. "That was a lot of nonsense. He could talk your arm off."

Hinkle, who was from Brownfield, Texas, taught Dean to ride herd and rope cattle, and even how to spot what area a Texan hailed from by the crease he wore in his hat. He and Dean also looked into a couple of oil deals together and made plans to enter a rodeo at the Cow Palace in San Francisco in the fall.

Jimmy practiced rope tricks Hinkle showed him. "I taught him how to build a loop with the rope," Hinkle said. "There's a lot more to it than just making a big loop. You have to work it so that you can throw it off your hand just right. Before we came back to Hollywood, Jimmy was an expert." Dean neatly employed his newly acquired skill in the movie; in a scene with Rock Hudson he nonchalantly performed a rope trick while delivering his lines; it stole the scene.

At sundown after a hard day on the set, Dean and Hinkle would climb into the company car and drive off into the prairie to hunt jackrabbits. Dean had bought an old miner's hat, and he used the beam on the hat to hunt in the dark. Often he and Hinkle remained out all night, returning to the location after dawn. Dean would later show up at breakfast and announce to the others: "We killed 34 rabbits last night; that makes a total of 104 to date"; then he'd turn and leave. "There were many things about this boy that many people wouldn't have overlooked," Henry Ginsberg, the film's coproducer, said later. "I overlooked them because he had talent."

But there was another side to Dean as well. One night he and Hinkle killed a coyote, and only 300 yards from where the coyote was shot they discovered a ewe and her lamb. Jimmy was deeply moved. "If we hadn't gotten the coyote," he told Hinkle, "it would have killed that lamb. Sure as shooting it would have killed that lamb."

A few weeks after he returned to Hollywood, Dean decided that he would never hunt again. He told a friend: "I'm not going to kill rabbits or birds or anything any more. They don't do anybody any harm."

Nor was Dean's capability for compassion only expressed in words. When actress Mercedes McCambridge suffered a mild case of sunstroke, Dean visited her hotel room every day to cheer her up, always admonishing her before he left, "Don't tell anybody I was here."

"I can't tell you how he needed to be patted," Miss McCambridge said afterward. "He was the runt in the litter of thoroughbreds. You could feel the loneliness beating out of him, and it hit you like a wave.

"You can forgive a lot of things for talent, and Jimmy was bursting with it."

Driving to location one morning outside of town, Dean came across an accident on Highway 90. A car had skidded off the road and rolled into a ditch, injuring the driver. Dean stopped and flagged down another car to get an ambulance. While waiting for the ambulance to arrive, he did his best to comfort the injured man, shielding his face from the sun with a straw hat.

The following Sunday, the Reverend Earl Zetsche, pastor of the First Christian Church of Marfa, said a special prayer of thanks for James Dean for helping save the life of another human being; a short time later the same congregation again said prayers for James Dean, this time because he had lost his own life in an automobile accident.

June had been hot in Marfa, but July was even hotter. By early morning the temperature was already in the 80's and in the afternoon the mercury climbed well past 90.

After four weeks of being on location, the cast had grown weary and restless. Despite the hospitality of Marfans, supper dances at the local Lions Club had no further allure, and the visitors yearned for the excitement of Hollywood.

After a final week of shooting in the broiling Texas sun, the last location footage was in the can, and by July 8 the company was free to depart. Two months of filming remained to be done back at the studio in Burbank, but the movie was right on schedule.

Chapter 14

In Hollywood, Dean quickly got back into the old grove, dropping by the Villa Capri for dinner his first night in town, and calling friends to let them know he was back. One girl he called for a date upon his arrival home was a shapely Swiss-born actress he had first met only the day before leaving for Texas. Her name was Ursula Andress, and she also was a friend of Dick Clayton's.

Later famous as a James Bond heroine, Ursula was then a nineteen-year-old starlet who had only recently arrived in this country and was under contract to Paramount. The studio had discovered her in Europe, where she had appeared in several Italian-made quickies like *The Many Loves of Casanova*. Until she learned to speak English better, Paramount was keeping her under wraps, hoping to eventually groom her as another Marlene Dietrich.

On their dirst date, Dean had come by for Ursula an hour late. "He come in room like wild animal and smell of everything I don't like," she complained in her German accent. "He stalked all through my house . . . then sat down on the sofa and sat staring at me saying nothing." When they started talking, they immediately got in an argument over music. "It was then I first felt like an American," Ursula later said. "In Europe a woman does not argue with a man."

They joined friends for dinner and afterward went to a club on Sunset Strip to hear some jazz. The band allowed Dean to sit in with them, and he spent most of the evening playing the drums. "I don't like to be alone, so I went home," Ursula said. About an hour later Dean drove up to her house on his motorcycle, and after apologizing, convinced her to go for hot chocolate. They came back to the house, and sitting on the curb, talked till 5:00 A.M.

That same day Dean left for Texas, but as soon as he returned to Hollywood he and Ursula picked up where they had left off.

"We would fight, then make up, then fight again," Ursula remembers. They argued about anything and everything, everywhere they went. Jimmy complained that Ursula's German Shepherd was eating him out of house and home. "It'd be cheaper to have a family," he told her. At the Villa Capri he objected when Ursula ordered steak. "It's costing me five dollars every time I take you out. Why can't you eat spaghetti for 65 cents?"

"We fight like cats and dogs. No—on second thought, like two monsters," Dean admitted. "But then we make up and it's fun. Ursula doesn't take any baloney from me and I don't take any from her. I guess it's because we're both so egotistical."

Ursula, however, wasn't the only female with whom Dean was having a personality conflict; for some time he and his landlady had been having a dispute over his odd hours and late-night bongo sessions, and Dean finally decided to move. Some months before, he had taken an option on Lana

Turner's former home atop Laurel Canyon, but changed his mind when a columnist printed an item about it and tourists began flocking to the site. Now he looked elsewhere.

Nicolas Romanos, the maitre d' at the Villa Capri, had recently put his home in the San Fernando Valley up for rent and moved to the beach, so that his wife, Grace, who was in poor health, could be near the ocean. Romanos had been having trouble renting his house, but as soon as Dean saw it he decided to take it.

The home, which was destroyed in a fire several years later, was located at 14611 Sutton Street in Sherman Oaks, a quiet residential neighborhood.

Built to resemble a hunting lodge, it had a large living room with a seven-foot stone fireplace, a small dining area, and a kitchen. There was no bedroom, but a small balcony that jutted out over the living room had a cot on which to sleep.

Dean signed a year's lease at $250 a month, also taking an option to buy the house within the year for $29,500.

The place had come furnished, but somehow everything in it seemed to fit its new tenant's personality to a tee: in the living room there was a white bearskin rug, an old-fashioned wheel lamp hanging from the high ceiling, and a huge bronze eagle Dean immediately dubbed "Irving." Dean was delighted with the home and took great pleasure in showing it off to friends, always demonstrating how he climbed into bed by means of a wooden ladder.

Otherwise, however, things were not going quite so well.

On *Giant* Stevens and Dean had not managed to resolve their differences, and to make things worse the director was faced with new problems as well. Elizabeth Taylor had suddenly been hospitalized for a blood clot on her leg, the result, she claimed, of having worn jodhpurs that were too tight for her. The blood clot proved not to be serious, and Stevens was able to shoot around her until she was released from the hospital.

But no sooner was she back at work than she suffered an attack of sciatica (severe backache) and had to be briefly hospitalized again. This time, however, Stevens did not learn of his star's hospitalization until he read about it in the papers, and when he did he was convinced it was psychosomatic. Stevens' diagnosis was backed up by several doctors, but even so, when Liz returned to the studio she had a nurse and wheelchair ready on the set if her pains returned. (Later, when she learned of Dean's death she broke down and was hospitalized a third time.)

Meanwhile, the situation between Stevens and Dean was deteriorating daily. The early flareups in Texas now seemed mild compared to the range war that was about to erupt.

Starting the last week in July, Dean had had a series of early-morning calls that required him to be at the studio at 6:30 A.M. and made up by 9:00 A.M. For several days he managed to show up on time and ready for work, but by the end of each day his scene still had not been shot. Upset, Dean complained to a friend that he had "sat for three days . . . like a bump on a log watching that big, lumpy Rock Hudson make love to Liz . . ."

Convinced that Stevens was trying to punish him

by deliberately postponing his scenes, Dean decided to boycott the studio and take a day off for each one he had sat idle.

The following morning, true to his word, he failed to show up for a scheduled scene. Frantically, the studio put in a call to his home and Dean promised to be right in. But he never made it, and his absence cost the studio thousands of dollars in wasted time.

Word of Dean's rebellion spread throughout Hollywood. Columnist Sheila Graham printed a detailed account of the incident, upbraiding Dean as "a young so-called star who after a year in pictures wants to teach, instead of learn." Even the studio's reaching Dean on the phone, she informed her readers, had been "no mean feat in itself, for Dean guards his . . . number with the same secrecy the government puts on its nuclear developments. And even when his right number is reached, he may let it ring for hours and never answer it. Maybe he just likes to hear bells ring."

At Warners Dean was given a firm dressing-down by Stevens, but apparently he was still not ready to capitulate; several days later Dean was back on the carpet again, this time for being late on the set.

He had been scheduled to do a scene with Mercedes McCambridge. Miss McCambridge had slipped in her tub that morning and had cut herself badly, requiring several stitches, but she still managed to make it to the studio on time. Then she and the rest of the cast had to wait for Dean. When he finally showed up, the director berated him for five full minutes in front of the entire company. Stevens lit into Dean for his "inconsideration" and told the young actor he had never seen anyone "go Hollywood" in such a short time. As Stevens stormed off the set, he vowed Dean would "never appear in another film I do."

Hedda Hopper, Dean's staunchest supporter, rallied to his aid. "Jimmy Dean was late for work one day and you'd have thought he'd committed a crime," she wrote in her column, assuring Stevens. "He's worth waiting for, and I'm predicting he'll steal the picture to prove it."

But the director's tirade worked; knowing when he was licked, Dean at last gave in, coming as close to apologizing as he ever would. "The trouble with me is I'm just dog-tired," he told Dorothy Manners. "Everybody hates me and thinks I'm a heel. They say I've gone Hollywood, but honest I'm just the same as when I didn't have a dime. I went right into *Giant* immediately after a long, hard schedule on *Rebel*. Maybe I'd just better go away for a while."

The rebellion quelled, and, Dean back in the fold, the director was quick to forgive. He denied Dean was on any blacklist for future movies. "A lot of stories going around have been built on minor things," Stevens told the Los Angeles *Mirror-News*. "The boy's so preoccupied, he's the kind that can be late even if he's right there on the set . . . But his work is wonderful," the director added. "Everything went fine when we shot all night at the Statler and Jimmy even showed up for makeup call fifteen minutes early."

Chapter 15

Having lost the battle as well as the war at Warners, Dean readily found a sanctuary in the quiet of his new house. Friends often dropped by for late-night talks or to drink wine and listen to records on the new hi-fi Dean had recently installed. Two large speakers hung down from the beamed ceiling; neighbors claimed the music could be heard five blocks away.

The refrigerator was well stocked with hams Uncle Marcus sent from the farm, and in the celler Dean was building a trophy room with the help of Nick Adams. Intense and ambitious, Adams was very much like Dean, and later went on to a successful career of his own, playing off-beat parts. He had hitchhiked to Hollywood at eighteen, determined to make it as an actor. "Some men bet on horses or dogs," he liked to say. "I gambled on myself."

On top of the television set in the living room was an imitation Oscar someone had swiped from the set of *A Star Is Born* and given Dean. Whenever he could, he liked to watch the *Bob & Ray Show*, having been a fan since their days on radio. Sol Saks, Dean's neighbor, let him use his swimming pool freely.

Mike Connolly, a magazine reporter who dropped

by to interview Dean early in August, was surprised to find him so friendly and relaxed. Dean put on a pot of coffee, meanwhile giving the customary tour of the premises, proudly pointing out the apple and lemon trees that bloomed in the backyard. When the reporter noticed a hangman's noose strung from a ceiling beam, and a sign—"We Also Remove Bodies" —tacked next to it, Dean chalked them up to "my macabre sense of humor."

They had a long talk about music over coffee. As they talked, Dean kept changing records on his hi-fi, going from Bartok to African chants to an old Jimmie Rogers record he had picked up in a second-hand shop.

"I collect everything from twelfth- and thirteenth-century music," he boasted proudly, "to the extreme moderns—you know, Schoenberg, Berg, Stravinsky. I also like Sinatra's 'Songs for Young Lovers' album."

Among Dean's closest friends there was now a growing feeling that somehow Jimmy had changed. One humid night, sitting in his kitchen with Lew Bracker, Dean turned to his friend and said quietly, "You know, Lew, I think we ought to get married."

"To each other?" Bracker joked.

"No. Seriously," Dean replied. "I mean it would be so right to come home to somebody who understands me, who cares."

Bracker, who is today a Los Angeles investment banker, was then living with his parents in Studio City, and to them Dean practically became one of the family that summer. "He'd come to the house," Bracker remembers, "with a bucket of peaches he'd picked from his tree for my mother. Or he'd bring a couple of pounds of hamburger and insist on cooking

157

dinner for us . . . At first, if we had other people in, he would sit in a corner of the yard by himself. But toward the end he was getting better . . . He'd join the other people and joke with them."

Dean's attitude toward Hollywood had softened too. There was now much surprise when Dean began showing up at the better-known night spots, or was seen around town escorting actresses like Leslie Caron. "Foreign girls intrigue me," Dean quipped.

When Ella Logan took over Ciro's to host a party for Sammy Davis, Jr., Dean dropped by and mingled easily with the other guests. At a private party given by Frank Sinatra at the Villa Capri in August for owner Patsy D'Amore, Jimmy came dressed in a suit, bringing Ursula as his date. He used the front door.

Yet, underneath it all, the rebellious spirit had not died entirely. In one of the last interviews he did, with a writer named Jan Jamison, Dean summed up his feelings, striking a note that might have served as an epitaph. "If a choice is in order—I'd rather have people hiss than yawn," Dean claimed. "Any public figure sets himself up as a target and that is the chance he takes. Most of us have more than one choice and I chose to be what I am, rather than remain a farm boy back in Indiana . . . Despite endless odds and issues along the way, I've never regretted it."

Writing that summer to his old friend, Reverend DeWeerd, Dean reached ever deeper inside himself. "I don't really know who I am, but it doesn't matter," he admitted. "There really isn't an opportunity for greatness in this world. We are impaled on a crock of conditioning. A fish that is in water has no choice that he is. Genius would have it that he swim in sand . . . We are fish and we drown."

But that summer Jimmy allowed himself little time for such melancholy thoughts. He was involved in a host of new activities, learning tennis, studying German ("so Ursula and I can fight better"), laying plans for the future.

In August Dean told friends that he hoped to form his own production company in the near future, working within Warners an an independent producer. He talked about doing a short of a Bartok ballet, *The Miraculous Mandarin* and wanted to film *The Little Prince*.

He had other ideas in mind as well: a life story of Tazio Nuvolari, the Italian racing ace who had been nicknamed "The Devil's Son," and a film on Billy the Kid. Dean said he would make the latter movie only "if I can do it honestly," portraying the outlaw as a cold-blooded killer rather than a romantic hero. In September Dean took a major step forward, putting writer John Wright to work on a prospective screen treatment.

The old spirit and drive had returned—to have tomorrow today, to live two years for every one.

On the set of *Giant* Dean became friendly with Sanford Roth, who had joined the company as still photographer after their return from Marfa. Roth, who died in 1962, was a former merchandising executive who had given up a successful business career to become a professional photographer. He and his wife Beulah had lived in Europe for a number of years, and he had done a book on Paris with Aldous Huxley.

When Dean learned Roth knew and collected the works of artists like Miro and Picasso, he asked: "When can I come and see you?" That same night he went to the Roths' West Hollywood home for dinner and stayed till five in the morning.

After that Dean was often in their company. He took them to the Villa Capri for dinner, and some evenings they would all go over to Will Wright's for ice cream. Whenever Mrs. Roth knew Dean was coming over, she liked to make what soon became his favorite snack: Jewish salami toasted on Italian pizza.

The Roths stimulated Dean's yen to travel and introduced him to the writings of avant-garde writers they admired: Genet, Curzio Malaparte, and Gerald Heard, the English scientist who was then living in Hollywood.

Along with Roth, Dean visited a Buddist temple in downtown Los Angeles, observing a class in kendo, the Japanese art of self-defense. Jimmy naturally became enthusiastic about learning the sport and wanted to take lessons.

When Roth mentioned that he knew of an old hotel in Venice in which Sarah Bernhardt once stayed, Dean insisted they drive out to see it at once. It was late at night, but they managed to rouse the desk clerk to show them the room. Dean was thrilled to sit on the bed in which the great Bernhardt had slept.

"He knew the world was round," Roth said, "but he never stopped trying to prove it to himself."

Early in September, Roth introduced Dean to Pegot Waring, the West Coast sculptress, and Dean asked her to take him on as a student. "Acting is just interpretation," he told her. "I want to create for myself."

After his third lesson, he wanted her to explain the technique sculptors used to carve Mt. Rushmore.

Dean worked on a bust of Elizabeth Taylor and one of Edna Ferber, who was in Hollywood checking on the progress of the movie. The frail, elderly novelist was captivated by Dean, calling him "utterly winning one moment, obnoxious the next."

"Your profile resembles that of John Barrymore," she told him, adding sadly and prophetically, "but then, your automobile racing will probably soon take care of that."

Chapter 16

By September the subject of racing was indeed very much on Dean's mind. So far he had kept his promise to Stevens, but Dean's impatience was growing. He had missed the Hansen Dam race in June and the Torrey Pines contest in July. Over Labor Day he had attended a race in Santa Barbara, watching Lew Bracker drive. As a favor to the car club, Dean had gone on Tom Harmon's KNX sports show to promote the event, but his heart was not in it. "I heard the program and nearly cringed in sympathy for Tom," said driver Jim Matthews. "Pulling words out of Dean was like pulling teeth. Tom was POed at Dean and furious with me for setting up the interview."

Dean had loaned Bracker his racing helmet for good luck, but his friend did not have one of his better days, finishing twenty-fifth in a field of thirty-nine. He was sixteenth in class F.

Back from Santa Barbara, Dean spoke constantly of racing and events he planned to enter once *Giant* was completed, as it soon would be. There was a rugged road race, the Carrena Americana Mexico, that Dean had set his sights on. The 2,000-mile race was run down the Pan American Highway, and simply to finish was an achievement. But the race was run irregularly; no definite date had been set for the next event, and in the meantime there were at least two club meets Dean planned to enter. The first was in Salinas, some 350 miles up the coast, on October 1; the other was in nearby Willow Springs. Dean sent in his entry to Salinas.

Since his return from Marfa back in July, Dean had been shopping for another car, one with more horsepower and a finer racing edge. He had put a small down payment on a Lotus Mark IX, a British racer, planning to install in it an Offenhauser engine.

But now, through Lew Bracker, he heard of another car, a Porsche 550 Spyder that Bracker had spotted in the window of Competition Motors on North Vine Street.

The car was a beauty. It cost $6,900 and was capable of 150 miles an hour. Its body was made of thin aluminum and had no windshield or bumpers; it had been designed specifically for the track.

Dean traded in his old Porsche Speedster, paying the difference. Before completing the deal, however, Dean insisted that Rolf Weutherich, a young mechanic at the shop, promise to accompany him to his next race and check the car before he competed. Weutherich, a thin former Luftwaffe pilot who had recently come to this country from Germany, readily agreed. The mechanic had seen Dean race and admired his driving. "He was one of the best drivers in California," Weutherich said. "He had that essential feel for fast cars and dangerous roads. When he drove, he drove with his whole being. He had steel in his hands."

The deal was completed the same morning Dean visited the shop. It was Monday, September 21.

The next two weeks were busy and crowded with activity. *Rebel Without a Cause* was sneak-previewed in Huntington Park and Jimmy went with several friends. "He was sitting there just behind me," Sal Mineo recalls, "and half a dozen times when he was really terrific I turned around to look at him. He was giving that grin of his and almost blushing, looking at the floor." Dean said he thought the movie was good but could have been better, and that he was dissatisfied by a number of his own scenes. Afterward, he told Dennis Stock he was a bit put off by Ray's Hitchcock-like appearance in the movie. In the film's final frame the director is seen walking toward the Planetarium with his back to the camera.

But for the moment Dean kept the comment to himself, and after the preview, Ray, Dean, Natalie, Mineo, and Nick Adams—the whole gang—went to Googie's to celebrate.

Largely as a favor to Lew Bracker, Dean had recently taken out a $100,000 life insurance policy with Bracker's company, Pacific Indemnity (American agents for Lloyds of London), and one afternoon Bracker brought the policy by the studio for the actor to sign. Dean signed the policy, telling Bracker he wanted the bulk of the money to go to his aunt and uncle, and the rest to be distributed among his relatives in Indiana. Bracker explained that he should make out a will, specifying each amount. Dean agreed, but never followed through, and on his death his entire estate went to his father.

Jane Deacy, Dean's agent, had come to town for several days on business, and Dean was happy to entertain her. He met her at the airport and filled her Chateau Marmont suite with flowers and candy.

Miss Deacy got right to work, negotiating a new contract for her client with Warners. Dean's base salary for *Giant* was $15,000—though an overtime clause raised the figure to nearly $30,000—but in the future he would receive $100,000 per film. The year 1956 was still to be open for Dean to do a Broadway play, and several offers were already being considered.

Miss Deacy had also lined up two television specials back in New York. One was a dramatization of *The Corn is Green* with Judith Anderson, to be done on NBC in late October. Dean was to play Morgan Evans, the young Oxford-bound coal miner's son. The other show was A.E. Hotchner's adaptation of the Hemingway short story, *The Battler*, in which Dean would play Ad Francis, the battered prizefighter. Arthur Penn had been signed to direct.

In addition, MGM had gotten Warners approval to borrow Dean for *Somebody Up There Likes Me*, which was scheduled to go before the cameras in January. Dean had read Graziano's book and liked it. "What a guy," Dean said. "One day when he was in the army, he got tired of it and just got up—walked out—went over the hill. The army never forgave him . . . You've got to admire that kind of nerve."

Dean met Dore Schary, the head of MGM, and the encounter went well. Schary told him he had in mind Nick Ray or Robert Wise as director, and Dean was happy about the possibility of working with Ray again. Schary also told Dean that Pier Angeli had been chosen to play Graziano's wife in the film, and Schary remembers the actor seemed very happy with the choice. Another friend, Sal Mineo, who had a cameo in *Giant*, was going to be in the cast as well.

Dean's future appeared secure. The American Sportswear Manufacturers Co. asked him to endorse a line of clothing, and he and Lew Bracker talked about obtaining a Porsche dealership, to be called Jimmy Dean Motors. Coulter & Gray, a Beverly Hills business management firm, was called in to help Dean handle his investments.

On Friday, September 23, Dean was having dinner as usual at the Villa Capri. Sir Alec Guinness, who had only arrived in Hollywood that day, was there, and Dean asked Sir Alec to join him. "You are my favorite actor. I'd like to meet you," Dean said. Sir Alec found Dean "very agreeable," and the two talked casually about actors and acting. Later Dean insisted on showing him his new Porsche, which was parked outside the restaurant. "When he told me the speed he wanted to go in it," Guinness remembers, "I begged him never to get into it. Something made me say: 'If you do, you will be dead in a week.'"

This was not the first premonitory warning, nor was it the last. Several days later Dean offered coproducer Henry Ginsberg a ride to the studio, and when Ginsberg got there, he told the production department: "If you have any loose ends, you better tie them up quick. The way this kid's handling that car I don't think he's going to be around much longer."

The next day Dean completed his work on *Giant*. This was the famous banquet scene in which Jett Rink collapses and passes out in front of a packed ballroom. To make him look older and more dissipated, Dean's hair had been shaved back and dyed gray. Dean kept missing his lines and the scene had to be reshot several times, until Stevens ordered it printed. Stevens, though, was still not satisfied with the print, and later, after Dean's death, Nick Adams was quietly brought in to dub additional dialogue.

But for Dean his commitment on *Giant* was officially over. He was now free to race.

Looking forward to the big event on Saturday, Jimmy invited several friends to go along with him, but for a while it didn't look as though he could get anyone to go. Nick Adams was leaving for New York to be with Natalie Wood, and Lew Bracker had tickets for the USC-Texas game. "Okay," Dean told him. "It's your funeral."

Bill Stevens told Dean he couldn't leave Friday morning as Dean planned, but would drive to Salinas himself that night and be there in time for the race the next day. Stevens was packing his bags for the trip when he learned of Dean's death. "If I was with him it wouldn't have happened," Stevens remembers sadly. "I never let him drive that way."

Finally, Dean convinced Bill Hickman to accompany him, and photographer Sandy Roth, who was doing a story on Dean for *Collier's*, agreed to go too.

On Wednesday, the 28th, Dean relaxed much of the day, then went to the movies that evening with Ursula and Lew Bracker to see *I Am a Camera*.

Thursday he drifted around town, appearing at Warners around noon in his car. He talked with Stevens a few minutes, then drove off, telling the director, "So long, I think I'll let the Spyder out."

For several days Dean had been toying with the idea of driving the car to Salinas himself instead of towing it on a trailer. Driving around Hollywood he had only managed to put a couple of hundred miles on the odometer, and Weutherich, his mechanic, felt he should have driven the car at least 500 miles to properly learn to handle it. Thursday Dean definitely decided to drive the car himself.

Late in the afternoon, Dean picked up Bill Hickman to drive down the coast to Santa Barbara to put more mileage on the car.

"In those final days racing was what he cared about most," remembers Hickman, who later did the stunt driving in *The French Connection*. "I had been teaching him things like how to put a car in a four-wheel drift, but he had plenty of skill of his own. If he had lived he might have become a champion driver. We had a running joke. I'd call him 'Little Bastard' and he'd call me 'Big Bastard.' I never stop thinking of those memories."

The car handled well on the road to Santa Barbara, but when the fog started rolling in from the ocean, Dean was forced to turn back. Driving back to town, a highway patrol car followed them for speeding, but the Porsche managed to outrun it.

That evening Dean stopped by the apartment of Jeanette Miller, a young actress who was another of Dick Clayton's clients and whom Dean sometimes dated when he and Ursula were on the outs. Several weeks before Elizabeth Taylor had given Dean a Siamese kitten, which he named Marcus. Because he was unable to look after it, Jeanette had agreed to take the kitten and Dean brought it over. Jeanette had been looking at an old movie on television, *The Boy With Green Hair*, but Jimmy was too restless to watch the picture. They talked for a while, and before leaving the apartment around 9:30, he wrote a formula for feeding Marcus on the back of an old envelope. Then he kissed Jeanette lightly on the forehead, scratched the kitten, and left.

When Dean got back to his house, he phoned his father and asked him if he wanted to attend the race. His father declined the invitation, but promised to drop by Competition Motors the next day, along with Dean's uncle, Charles Nolan, who was visiting from Indiana. Too keyed-up to sleep, Dean drove his Porsche up to Coldwater Canyon and rode around for several hours, before finally returning home to bed.

The next day, Jimmy had a date with destiny.

Early Friday morning Dean was awakened by Nicolas Romanos, who often dropped by to fix breakfast and straighten up the house. The actor was still groggy from lack of sleep the night before.

"He didn't say hello," Romanos remembered. "He never would. He kept his drums at the bottom of the stairs and he would sit down and beat them. He would never talk until the coffee was ready."

Dean left the house at 7:45, dressed in bluejeans and a T-shirt. Romanos stayed behind to clean up and put the breakfast dishes away.

It was already a warm morning. Dean drove his car slowly to Hollywood. On the side of the Porsche he had painted his racing number, 130, and had written across the rear the nickname "The Little Bastard."

Dean was at Competition Motors by 8:00. According to Aljean Meltsir, who wrote a detailed account of that day, Weutherich went immediately to work, checking the Porsche over. Dean packed the floor, then came over and asked the mechanic if he needed help. "No thanks," Weutherich joked. "You'll only complicate things."

Dean went into the office and thumbed through a

newspaper, but within a few minutes he was back, looking impatiently over Weutherich's shoulder.

When the mechanic had finished checking the car, he attached a safety belt across the driver's seat. Since Dean was going to be alone during the race, he didn't fix one for the passenger's seat. Dean sat in the car and tried the belt.

Around ten o'clock Hickman and Roth showed up at the shop. They were going to take Dean's station wagon on the trip. The mechanic would ride in the Porsche with Dean.

A few minutes later, Dean's father and uncle walked in. Jimmy offered to take his uncle for a ride, and they drove around the block a couple of times.

At noon Weutherich went home to change clothes, and Dean and the others went to the Hollywood Ranch Market, half a block away, for coffee and doughnuts.

When they got back to the shop, Dean told his father he had an extra ticket if he wanted to see the race, but Winton was unable to make the trip; several hours later when Dean's body was taken from the wreckage he still had the ticket in his pocket.

At one-thirty they were at last ready to leave. Winton and Jimmy's uncle drove off. Roth photographed Dean and Weutherich as they sat in the car, hands clasped above their heads in a victory salute.

Traffic was heavy as the two cars drove out to Ventura Boulevard toward Highway 99, which cuts through the mountains between Los Angeles and Bakersfield.

The sun was high in the afternoon sky. Sometimes the Porsche led, sometimes the station wagon moved out in front as they headed for the open road.

Dean smoked cigarette after cigarette which Rolf

170

lit for him, all the while pumping the mechanic with questions about how the car was operating.

Rolf finally closed his eyes against the sun's glare and leaned his head back, almost lulled to sleep by the soft purr of the motor.

Dean was happy behind the wheel. The wind rushed by as the low car hugged the open road. "Life is wonderful," Dean is supposed to have murmured.

A few minutes before 3:00 they stopped near the top of Ridge Route at a roadside place for something to eat. Dean had a glass of milk and Rolf ordered a dish of ice cream. The mechanic warned Jimmy not to go too fast during the race the next day. "Don't try to win," he told him. "It's a big jump from a Speedster to a Spyder. Try for second or third. Drive for the experience."

"All right," Dean replied. "You give me the pit signals."

A few minutes later Roth and Hickman came in and ordered sandwiches. When they finished eating, they all left the restaurant.

Back on the highway, the Porsche was quickly in the lead. A highway patrol officer, O.V. Hunter, flagged down the car for speeding. Dean was given a ticket for doing 65 miles an hour in a 45-mile-an-hour zone. Roth and Hickman, who had pulled up alongside in the station wagon, also were given a summons.

Before they drove off, Dean and the others decided their next stop would be for dinner in Paso Robles, 130 miles away.

From then on, the station wagon was never again in the lead.

As Dean approached Blackwell's Corners, a gas station-general store an hour away, he spotted a

Mercedes 300-SL and pulled off the road to examine it. The car belonged to Lance Reventlow, Barbara Hutton's son, who was also on his way to the meet, along with race driver Bruce Kessler. Jimmy and the two drivers talked for a while; they too had been ticketed for speeding earlier. It had been a busy afternoon for the highway patrol.

Before the two left, Dean told Kessler that he had hit 100 miles an hour on the open stretch of road between Bakersfield and the Corners.

Roth and Hickman arrived in the station wagon. Roth bought a bag of apples for the road. "How do you like the Spyder now?" Dean asked, his face flushed from the sun. "I want to keep this car for a long time—a real long time."

Dean smoked a last cigarette and got back into the Porsche; his safety belt remained unfastened.

"See you in Paso Robles," he yelled to Roth.

On Highway 66 Dean headed west, toward the ocean. The setting sun loomed over the mountains in the distance, shining in Dean's eyes. The narrow road was deserted. Dean pressed on, wanting to feel the car's speed. The Porsche hugged the road, its silver body, the traditional German racing color, blending into the desert.

At a narrow intersection in the road, ten miles from Blackwell's Corners, where Highway 466 meets Highway 41, a Ford, driven by a young college student from Tulare named Donald Turnupseed, prepared to turn.

Dean saw the car too late, crying out as it hurled into them. The impact threw Weutherich nineteen feet from the car. His jaw was broken and his hip fractured in several places, but he recovered months later.

Turnupseed was uninjured and was later absolved from blame.

Dean's neck was broken on impact and his chest crushed where the steering wheel smashed into him.

He had been killed instantly. It was 5:45 P.M.

On October 8 funeral services were held at the Friends Church in Fairmount, where Dean had worshipped as a boy.

Some 3,000 people, more than the entire population of the town, turned out to pay their last respects. The church was filled with family and friends, and hundreds of others gathered outside.

There was very little evidence of Hollywood glitter. Henry Ginsberg was there representing the cast of *Giant* and Elizabeth Taylor had sent an arrangement of orchids. The accompanying card said simply, "With love always, Elizabeth." Ginsberg told the townfolks that Dean "was not only well liked, but highly respected by his fellow workers in the movie industry. He was adjusting himself well to his sudden rise to stardom."

A handful of Dean's personal friends—Lew Bracker, Nick Adams, and Dennis Stock—came to say goodbye.

The Quaker service was a simple one. The Reverend James DeWeerd, Dean's boyhood friend, read a brief eulogy. "We cannot measure a life in years, moments, days, or minutes," he said. "Although Jimmy's life was a short one, he accomplished more than most persons do if they live to be 70 or 80."

173

The organist played "Going Home" from the New World Symphony, and as the service ended, Dean's body was borne from the church. Five young men with whom he had played basketball in high school served as pallbearers.

The first chill of autumn in the Indiana air, James Byron Dean was buried beside his mother in a small cemetery at the edge of a cornfield, a quiet resting place that had once been an Indian burial ground.

Debts and Acknowledgments

Much of the material in this book is based on personal reminiscences, and I would like to thank the following people who talked to me about Dean or wrote letters, and in some cases did both: Eddie Albert, Jean Alexander, Joseph Anthony, Margaret Barker, Barbara Baxley, James Bellah, Dr. Joseph B. Birdsell, Dr. Walden P. Boyle, Lew Bracker, Rogers Brackett, Frank Burns, Lon Chapman, David Clarke, Jeff Corey, Frank Corsaro, Sanger Crumpaker, Marion Daugherty, Ann Doran, Jeanette Miller Doty, Abe Feder, Paul Fix, Constance Ford, Henry Ginsberg, Ruth Goetz, Manuel Gonzales, Michael Gordon, Richard Grayson, Sir Alec Guinness, Pat Hardy, Matt Harlib, Julie Harris, Terese Hayden, Claire Heller, Franklin Heller, Robert Heller, Michael Higgens, George Roy Hill, Pat Hingle, John Houseman, Gusti Huber, Paul Huber, Anne Jackson, Billy James, Edgar Kahn, John Kalin, Lili Kardell, Elia Kazan, Bruce Kessler, Archer King, Martin Kingsley, Dane Knell, Tony Krabner, Piper Laurie, Ralph Levy, Jerry Lucce, Salem Ludwig, Sidney Lumet, John Lund, Daniel Mann, Arlene Sachs Martell, Sal Mineo, Terry Moore, Ann McCormack, Clyde McCullough, Adeline Nall, William F. Nolan,

Mrs. Gene N. Owen, Betsy Palmer, Arthur Penn, Nehemiah Persoff, Dan Petrie, John Peyser, Arthur Pierson, Doris Quinlan, Ronald Reagan, Nicolas Romanos, Walter Ross, Beulah Roth, Howard Sackler, Sol Saks, Roy Schatt, Dore Schary, William Self, James Sheldon, Elizabeth Sheridan, Irving Shulman, Herman Shumlin, Robert Simon, Sidney Skolsky, Rusty Slocum, Leonard Spiegelgass, Bill Stevens, John Stix, Dennis Stock, Ernie Stockert, Lee Strasberg, Arnold Sundgaard, Florence Sundstrom, Lela Swift, Larry Swindell, Marc Towers, Eli Wallach, James Wasson, Ruth Waterbury, Paul Weaver, Christine White, Alec Wilder, Ortense Winslow.

The following individuals provided background material, or helped with the project in other ways, checking facts, suggesting possible leads, in many instances taking time from their own busy schedules to lend their support: Ted Ashton, formerly of Warner Brothers Publicity Dept.; Jay Barney; John Behrens of CBS; Connie Berman and Bernadette Carrozza of Macfadden-Bartell Publications; Betty Ann Besch; Fred Coe; William Collins of the Philadelphia *Inquirer*; Earl Conrad; C. Ray Cooper, Registrar of Santa Monica Junior College; Norman Corwin; Robert J. Costomiris; Pascal Covici, Jr.; John Crowell, researcher at the California State Library (Sacramento); Peggy Cummings, of the UCLA Alumni and Development Center; Digby Diehl of the Los Angeles *Times*; Richard H. Dodge, Publications Adviser, Santa Monica Junior College; Mrs. Geraldine Duclow of the Philadelphia Free Library Theater Collection; George Eells; Morris L. Ernst; Jack Garfein of the Actor &

Director's Lab (Los Angeles); Jay Glass; Chandler Harris, Public Information Manager (UCLA); Don Herbert; Barbara Hillman of the Dallas *Morning News*; Lee Israel; Hilary James and Bill Latham of Warner Brothers; Chris Kager of the New York Mets; Phil Lyman of the Gotham Book Mart; Mrs. Emma Mallan, former owner of the Paisano Hotel, Marfa, Texas; Gloria Mariano; Armina Marshall of the Theater Guild; Charles Martyn of the Philadelphia *Evening Bulletin*; Jerry Mastoli; Jim Matthews, historian of the California Sports Car Club; Worthington Miner and J.P. Nickel, formerly of Studio One; Dr. Paul Myers and the staff of the Theater Collection of the New York Public Library; Mrs. Ann McCallum of the Marfa, Texas, Chamber of Commerce; Barry McCarthy; Norma Nannini of *Variety*; Vivian Nathan; Terry Ork; Martin Quigley, Jr.; Bonnie Rothbart of the library of the Academy of Motion Picture Arts and Sciences (Los Angeles); Andrew Sarris; Eileen Shanahan; Charles Silver of the Museum of Modern Art Film Library (New York); Elaine Steinbeck; Selma Tembler; Howard Thompson of *The New York Times*; Lou Valentino of Time, Inc.; Jerry Vermilye of *TV Guide*; Frank Wetzel of the New York Alumni Chapter of Sigma Nu; Martha Wright of the Indiana State Library (Indianapolis).

I would also like to thank Robert Chuter for making available to me numerous items from his vast collection of Dean memorabilia. David Garfield allowed me access to his own work in progress dealing with a history of the Actors Studio and helped me track down Dean's work there, which I might have otherwise overlooked. I am indebted to Carl Himmel for translating Kurt Kuberzig's *Vom Film Fur Fans* (1962). Beverly Linet kindly shared with me her own store of knowledge gathered as a Hollywood correspondent in the 1950's. Leslie Aquaviva aided me with my research in Los Angeles and helped make my stay there a pleasant one.

Two friends, William Bostock and Robert Hubbard, read the book in manuscript and made a number of valuable suggestions.

At Pinnacle Michael Hayes, Ann Kearns, Barbara Leighton, Eileen Schary, and Ronni Lee Tropp gave encouragement and support, without which this book might not have been finished. Last but not least, I would like to thank my publisher, David Zentner, my aunt and friend Helen DeLouise, and my parents, who helped make this and so many other things a reality.

About the Author

Ronald Martinetti is a former book columnist for *Newsday*, the Long Island newspaper. Before that, he wrote for the *Wall Street Journal*, where an editor described him as being "argumentative, temperamental, and not a good bet for future employment."

Bibliography

Allan, James B. *Elizabeth Taylor*. Derby, Conn.: Monarch Books, 1961.

Backus, Jim. *Rocks on the Roof*. New York: G. P. Putnam's Sons, 1958.

Bast, William. *James Dean*. New York: Ballantine Books, 1956.

Beaton, Cecil. *Cecil Beaton's Fair Lady*. New York: Holt, 1964.

Conrad, Barnaby. *Matador*. Boston: Houghton, Mifflin, 1952.

Conrad, Earl. *Billy Rose: Manhattan Primitive*. Cleveland: World Publishing Co., 1968.

Dos Passos, John. *Midcentury*. Boston: Houghton, Mifflin, 1961.

Ellis, Royston. *Rebel*. London: Consul Books, 1962.

Ferber, Edna. *A Kind of Magic*. Garden City: Doubleday, 1963.

Goodman, Ezra. *The Fifty-Year Decline and Fall of Hollywood*. New York: Simon & Schuster, 1961.

Gottlieb, Polly Rose. *The Nine Lives of Billy Rose*. New York: Crown, 1968.

Hopper, Hedda (with James Brough). *The Whole Truth and Nothing But*. Garden City: Doubleday, 1963.

Hyams, Joe. *Mislaid in Hollywood*. New York: Peter H. Wyden, 1973.

Kael, Pauline. *I Lost It at the Movies*. Boston: Little, Brown and Company, 1965.

Morella, Joe, and Epstein, Edward Z. *Brando: The Unauthorized Biography*. New York: Crown, 1973.

Morin, Edgar. *The Stars*. New York: Grove Press, 1960.

Rivkin, Allen, and Kerra, Laura (editors). *Hello, Hollywood!* Garden City: Doubleday, 1962.

Ross, Walter. *The Immortal*. New York: Simon & Schuster, 1958.

Saint-Exupéry, Antione de. *The Little Prince*. New York: Harcourt, Brace and World, 1943.

Salgues, Yves. *James Dean: ou le Mal de vivre*. Paris: Pierre Horay, 1957.

Sarris, Andrew. *Interviews with Film Directors*. Indianapolis: Bobbs-Merrill, 1968.

Tanner, Louise. *Here Today*. New York: Thomas Y. Crowell, 1959.

Taylor, Elizabeth. *Elizabeth Taylor: An Informal Memoir*. New York: Harper, 1965.

Thomas, T. T. *I, James Dean*. New York: Popular Library, 1957.

INDEX

182